DEFEATING TERRORISM IN SYRIA:
A NEW WAY FORWARD

HEARING

BEFORE THE

SUBCOMMITTEE ON TERRORISM,
NONPROLIFERATION, AND TRADE

OF THE

COMMITTEE ON FOREIGN AFFAIRS
HOUSE OF REPRESENTATIVES

ONE HUNDRED FIFTEENTH CONGRESS

FIRST SESSION

FEBRUARY 14, 2017

Serial No. 115–3

Printed for the use of the Committee on Foreign Affairs

Available via the World Wide Web: http://www.foreignaffairs.house.gov/ or
http://www.gpo.gov/fdsys/

U.S. GOVERNMENT PUBLISHING OFFICE

24–241PDF   WASHINGTON : 2017

For sale by the Superintendent of Documents, U.S. Government Publishing Office
Internet: bookstore.gpo.gov   Phone: toll free (866) 512–1800; DC area (202) 512–1800
Fax: (202) 512–2104   Mail: Stop IDCC, Washington, DC 20402–0001

COMMITTEE ON FOREIGN AFFAIRS

EDWARD R. ROYCE, California, *Chairman*

CHRISTOPHER H. SMITH, New Jersey
ILEANA ROS-LEHTINEN, Florida
DANA ROHRABACHER, California
STEVE CHABOT, Ohio
JOE WILSON, South Carolina
MICHAEL T. McCAUL, Texas
TED POE, Texas
DARRELL E. ISSA, California
TOM MARINO, Pennsylvania
JEFF DUNCAN, South Carolina
MO BROOKS, Alabama
PAUL COOK, California
SCOTT PERRY, Pennsylvania
RON DeSANTIS, Florida
MARK MEADOWS, North Carolina
TED S. YOHO, Florida
ADAM KINZINGER, Illinois
LEE M. ZELDIN, New York
DANIEL M. DONOVAN, JR., New York
F. JAMES SENSENBRENNER, JR.,
  Wisconsin
ANN WAGNER, Missouri
BRIAN J. MAST, Florida
FRANCIS ROONEY, Florida
BRIAN K. FITZPATRICK, Pennsylvania
THOMAS A. GARRETT, JR., Virginia

ELIOT L. ENGEL, New York
BRAD SHERMAN, California
GREGORY W. MEEKS, New York
ALBIO SIRES, New Jersey
GERALD E. CONNOLLY, Virginia
THEODORE E. DEUTCH, Florida
KAREN BASS, California
WILLIAM R. KEATING, Massachusetts
DAVID N. CICILLINE, Rhode Island
AMI BERA, California
LOIS FRANKEL, Florida
TULSI GABBARD, Hawaii
JOAQUIN CASTRO, Texas
ROBIN L. KELLY, Illinois
BRENDAN F. BOYLE, Pennsylvania
DINA TITUS, Nevada
NORMA J. TORRES, California
BRADLEY SCOTT SCHNEIDER, Illinois
THOMAS R. SUOZZI, New York
ADRIANO ESPAILLAT, New York
TED LIEU, California

AMY PORTER, *Chief of Staff*   THOMAS SHEEHY, *Staff Director*

JASON STEINBAUM, *Democratic Staff Director*

———

SUBCOMMITTEE ON TERRORISM, NONPROLIFERATION, AND TRADE

TED POE, Texas, *Chairman*

JOE WILSON, South Carolina
DARRELL E. ISSA, California
PAUL COOK, California
SCOTT PERRY, Pennsylvania
LEE M. ZELDIN, New York
BRIAN J. MAST, Florida
THOMAS A. GARRETT, JR., Virginia

WILLIAM R. KEATING, Massachusetts
LOIS FRANKEL, Florida
BRENDAN F. BOYLE, Pennsylvania
DINA TITUS, Nevada
NORMA J. TORRES, California
BRADLEY SCOTT SCHNEIDER, Illinois

(II)

CONTENTS

DEFEATING TERRORISM IN SYRIA: A NEW WAY FORWARD

TUESDAY, FEBRUARY 14, 2017

House of Representatives,
Subcommittee on Terrorism, Nonproliferation, and Trade,
Committee on Foreign Affairs,
Washington, DC.

The subcommittee met, pursuant to notice, at 2:01 p.m., in room 2172, Rayburn House Office Building, Hon. Ted Poe (chairman of the subcommittee) presiding.

Mr. POE. The subcommittee will come to order.

Without objection, all members may have 5 days to submit statements, questions, extraneous materials for the record, subject to the length limitation in the rules.

I will make my opening statement at this time.

The Syrian war has raged for nearly 6 years. Syria is in chaos. Terrorists, foreign fighters, rebels, foreign governments, all are engaged in battle for territory and control of different aspects of Syria.

On the screen—let's go back to the previous screen—you will see different areas of Syria. And the different areas that are controlled by ISIS is in the dark section.

Let's flip to the next screen quickly. I don't know if you can read that or not. There should be—for at least the panel in front of you, you should have the different actors, the state actors on one side and then the nonstate actors on the other.

The state actors are divided into pro-Assad and actors that are opposed to Assad, with the Middle Eastern countries at the top of each list, and then you have non-Middle Eastern countries at the bottom of each list. And you can see that there are numerous countries aligned on both sides.

And then there are nonstate actors that are involved, and those are a multitude of groups. They call themselves different things at different times. Some are terrorist groups. Some claim not to be terrorist groups that are terrorist groups.

One of the biggest things that I think we should know is that we have terrorist groups on both sides. We have Hezbollah on one side, which is obviously a terrorist group fighting for Assad; and we have ISIS on the other side that is a terrorist group. Al-Qaeda is a terrorist group, and they are also somewhat aligned with the anti-Assad group.

You have a multitude of actors all seeking their own self-interest in Syria. And this hearing is about really what do we see hap-

(1)

pening not only now but, hopefully, what is the end game after 6 years of war.

The losers in this have been the Syrian people, and I think they will continue to be the losers because, as the war rages, the war affects them more than anyone else. Half a million Syrian people have died, at least, in this war. And I don't call it a conflict; I call it a war. When you start dropping bombs on people, that is not a conflict, that is a war. Fifty thousand of those people, by all estimates, have been children. Five million Syrians have become refugees; 6 million are internally displaced. So that has been about 11 percent of the Syrian population killed or injured since the start of the violence.

The perpetrator of all of this sits directly at the regime of Bashar Assad and his backers in Moscow and Tehran. Assad has pursued a policy of murdering anybody that expresses criticism of his power. He uses barrel bombs, and it doesn't make any difference who those barrel bombs fall on as long as he thinks they are opposed to his regime.

Russia intervened in Syria in September 2015 and began air strikes against what it called terrorist targets. The Russians apparently are not very good in their targeting because it seems as though they have killed thousands of people in Syria and they haven't all been terrorists. The Syrian Network for Human Rights suggested last year that Russian strikes killed more Syrians than ISIS members.

Iran's terrorist proxy, Hezbollah, has also bloodied its hands in Syria. Since 2013, Hezbollah has operated openly in Syria, killing on behalf of the Assad regime. It has also created in Syria a perfect environment for out-of-towners, as I call them, who show up with their own self-interest, including terrorist groups. ISIS is there, and while ISIS no longer controls as much territory as they did in 2014, they still control major aspects of the Syrian population centers.

I have furnished each of our panelists a map, and there is also a map on the wall. Due to time constraints, I can't go into all of the details. But the thin black line in the middle of Syria and in the southern part of Syria is what is controlled by ISIS. The Kurds control the northern purple area. The yellow area is controlled by al-Qaeda and so-called Syrian dissidents and rebel groups. And then Assad controls the pink area to the west.

The questions to be asked today are: What is going to happen in the end game? What is the end game? And, also, I would like to know from our panelists, what is the national security interest of the United States? Should we ratchet it up? Should we do what we are doing now, which is kind of the Vietnam syndrome? Or should we leave it to the Middle East to resolve this conflict themselves? I would like the opinion of all three panelists to those three questions.

And I will turn it over to the gentleman from Massachusetts, who has fled to Washington to get out of the snow, for his opening statement.

Mr. KEATING. Thank you, Chairman Poe. And thank you for holding this hearing today.

The situation we have watched unfold in Syria the last 6 years has been wrought with complexities and, the chairman and I agree, with chaos and atrocities under the Assad government. Today, the war and the resulting humanitarian crisis is nothing short of a global tragedy.

So I am grateful for the attendance of our witnesses—Mr. Hassan, Ambassador Hof, Ms. Dalton—for their valuable insight into the ongoing political strife and challenges that the international community as well as the new administration faces in the months and years ahead.

If we are going to be smart about terrorism and specifically the rising role of ISIL, then we must first come to terms with the reality that their model of terrorism is built on a foundation of radicalization. To continue fighting ISIL in the battlefield requires that we recognize this pattern of recruitment and evolution in fighting tactics.

As we make progress in diminishing their territory, we must be mindful of their shifts in strategy to prioritize covert radicalization rather than maintain geographic strongholds. It becomes essential that we engage in this war of ideas by providing potential recruits with a choice of narratives. Those choices should include a path forward other than terrorism.

But, even more importantly, we must recognize that strengthening the resiliency and stability of communities is necessary for eradicating terrorism. And when families live in fear and when no one is accountable for keeping them safe and protecting their freedom, we will never be able to eliminate the conditions that produce these terrorists.

Countering ISIL in Syria, however, cannot be viewed as a one-dimensional prospect. Preventing attacks and limiting ISIL's capacity to operate within its network caliphates are also crucial to eliminating the terrorist threat there.

The U.S. cannot do this alone, nor should we. But we should also be wary of the compromises we are being asked to make, allegedly in the name of securing peace and combating terrorism.

I have grave concerns about the role of Russia and Iran and what they intend to play in countering ISIL and preventing future terrorists. Left without proper oversight or debate, this same Congress may 5, 10, or 15 years from now preside over a hearing of the same subject, examining how a Russian- and Iranian-led resolution to this crisis allowed ISIL to survive and become embedded in the region, like other terrorist groups which continue to pose a threat to the U.S. today.

For the time being, I believe we still have strong allies in Europe and the Middle East whose interests align with ours and who can make valuable contributions, along with our own, to tackle this threat. Our existing partnerships on intelligence-sharing, security, military strategy are robust, and we are united with our allies along a common goal for a peaceful resolution to this gruesome conflict and a stable political outcome for the people of Syria.

Even with close partnerships, there is still room for even stronger, more effective cooperation to close some of the gaps and inconsistencies that ISIL continues to exploit. With all the progress in the past decades to cement effective security partnerships among the U.S. and our allies, there is now a sound foundation to build upon that, together, we can isolate and destroy these terrorist threats. Neglecting these partnerships and incredible assets in the fight against terrorism would be a costly mistake.

Countering terrorism in Syria is a complex, multifaceted issue. If we fail to craft a comprehensive plan to address it, aspects of our national security will be compromised.

I look forward to the witnesses' testimony today and hearing from you on how to balance these diverse and sometimes seemingly divergent considerations when attempting to combat ISIL in Syria.

I yield back.

Mr. Poe. I thank the gentleman from Massachusetts.

The Chair will recognize members for 1-minute opening statements, and the Chair will follow the 60-minute—60-second rule, not 60 minutes.

The gentleman from South Carolina is recognized for 1 minute.

Mr. Wilson. Thank you, Mr. Chairman, Judge Poe.

And he and I worked together very closely on the 60-second rule, I can assure you.

But I want to thank the chairman for having such distinguished witnesses. And, already, this has been a helpful hearing to me, the map showing the level of control, how narrow it is, Damascus, west and north, but also to see the success of the Kurdish regional efforts from Iraq.

It is very important to me that we support the people of the Kurdish region, with the understanding that they are working to maintain and build a stable Iraq, and by doing that, by not indicating—expanding beyond the borders. But they are very successful. And that was very instructive to me, so I am very, very hopeful.

Additionally, I look forward to hearing of your efforts regarding counterpropaganda.

Thank you. And I, within the 60 seconds, hereby yield the balance of my time.

Mr. Poe. I thank the gentleman.

The Chair recognizes the gentleman from Illinois, Mr. Schneider.

Mr. Schneider. Thank you, Chairman Poe, Ranking Member Keating, for convening this important hearing.

And thank you to the witnesses for providing your expertise to inform this incredibly important discussion.

I hope that we all came here today with the recognition that Syria must be a priority for the new administration. With 5 million refugees and 6 million internally displaced people and more than 500,000 mostly civilians killed, the 6-year civil war is the greatest humanitarian crisis of the new century.

Syria borders key American allies, namely Israel, Jordan, and Turkey. The civil war is putting extreme pressure on the bordering states as well as the European nations. For 6 years, the situation has only gotten worse.

I hope our witnesses can shed light on how to neutralize and defeat the terrorist groups ISIS and Jabhat Fateh al-Sham, while at the same time working toward a political solution for the country that does not include Bashar al-Assad or cede control of Syria to

Iran and its proxy Hezbollah nor lead to further instability and the consequent return of terrorist groups.

As you have all shared in your testimony, there are no easy solutions or even mostly good choices, but walking away is clearly not an option.

Mr. POE. I thank the gentleman.

The Chair recognizes the gentleman from California, Mr. Cook.

Mr. COOK. Thank you very much, Mr. Chairman. I think this is a great hearing.

The problem that I have always with this is that every 6 months, a year, the players, the situation changes. And for us to get a grasp on this, it is almost impossible. We just had a similar hearing in the House Armed Services Committee, a different approach.

And I did want to thank Ambassador Hof for his service in Vietnam, where you were awarded the Purple Heart. I understand that you were involved in the 1983 investigation of the bombing of the Marine barracks, 1st Battalion, 8th Marines. That was my—I was not with them. That was my former battalion. And what happened then still lingers, and I hope we can go back to some of the causes as they relate to today.

I yield back. Thank you.

Mr. POE. I thank the gentleman.

Mr. Rohrabacher from California.

Mr. ROHRABACHER. Thank you very much, Mr. Chairman.

When we talk about ½ million people who are dead and have been killed in this, let's just admit this isn't just Assad. We keep saying Assad killed all these people. The fact is, if you look at our allies, whether it be Turkey, Saudi Arabia, Qatar, even the UAE, and certainly Iran, who is not an ally but in that region, any of those countries, any of those governments that faced an insurgency that kept on being financed over and over again would kill that many people. Assad is no different than the other dictators, yet we have insisted that he has to go. And, thus, the conflict goes on, and more and more people are made refugees and killed.

Who is at fault? I think we should stick our nose out of this and let them have, yes, Assad and their dictators in all the rest of these countries, and the United States shouldn't keep these conflicts going on and on and on.

Thank you.

Mr. POE. I thank the gentleman.

Anybody else wish to make an opening statement?

The Chair recognizes Ms. Titus.

Ms. TITUS. Well, thank you very much, Mr. Chairman, Ranking Member.

You know, throughout the campaign, we heard from candidate Trump that he knew more than the generals and he had a secret plan for fighting ISIS. Now, apparently, he has gone to the Pentagon to ask for some assistance.

As we go through this hearing, I would be curious to know what you all think about his willingness or ability to stick with a plan if we come up with it or if our policy is just going to jump from tweet to tweet.

Thank you.

Mr. POE. The Chair will now introduce all three witnesses and then——

Mr. GARRETT. Mr. Chairman?

Mr. POE. Yes.

Mr. GARRETT. If I might? I had not originally not intended to make introductory remarks.

Mr. POE. The Chair recognizes for 1 minute.

Mr. GARRETT. Thank you, Mr. Chairman, Ranking Member.

The comments by the gentleman from California sort of stir where I am on this. I think that this Nation would be well-advised never to arm any entity without having an easily articulable plan for an end state that is preferable to the current status quo.

And while Assad certainly has blood on his hands, I can't find, nor could former Secretary of State John Kerry, the Free Syrian Army. I couldn't tell you who leads it, which leaves us with two alternative solutions to the Assad problem, that being Jabhat al-Nusra or Jabhat Fateh al-Sham or ISIS, neither of which, I think, are a preferable option to a dictator in Assad, who has provided some level of stability, created a circumstance wherein 51 percent of college graduates in Syria are women and a safe zone for individuals of ethnic and religious minorities.

I would yield back the balance of my time.

Mr. POE. I thank the gentleman.

The Chair will now introduce the witnesses.

Mr. Hassan is a senior fellow at the Tahrir Institute for Middle East Policy. He is co-author of "ISIS: Inside the Army of Terror," a New York Times bestseller.

Ambassador Frederic Hof is the director of the Rafik Hariri Center for the Middle East at the Atlantic Council. Previously, Ambassador Hof served as Special Coordinator for the State Department's Office of the Special Envoy for Middle East Peace.

Ms. Melissa Dalton is a senior fellow and the deputy director of the International Security Program at CSIS. Her research focuses on U.S. defense policy in the Middle East, global U.S. defense strategy, and security cooperation with U.S. allies.

Mr. Hassan, we will start with you.

Each of you have 5 minutes. When you see the red light, stop talking.

Mr. Hassan.

STATEMENT OF MR. HASSAN HASSAN, SENIOR FELLOW, THE TAHRIR INSTITUTE FOR MIDDLE EAST POLICY

Mr. HASSAN. Thank you very much, Chairman Poe and members of the subcommittee. It is a privilege to present today here my views on Syria and terrorism.

I want to basically give, like, an optimistic view first. Despite the grim situation inside Syria, I think the U.S. Government has an opportunity to stem the challenges presented by the two international terrorist organizations operating in Syria, the Islamic State and al-Qaeda.

In fact, I would argue that the United States has more options or options it didn't necessarily have 2 years ago, including a way to prevent not only the Islamic State and al-Qaeda from operating in Syria or weakening both of them but also other radical groups from operating in at least 50 to 60 percent of Syria. The territory I am talking about includes areas that the Islamic State controls or once controlled since 2014.

You know, the way ISIS does things is, when they take an area, they act as a washing powder, I would say, which is basically to eradicate any Islamist and jihadist cells operating in the areas where they operate, because they want to prevent any support system for their rivals.

So they have done that in 50 to 60 percent of Syria—or 50 percent of Syria, to be more precise. So for al-Qaeda now to go back and fill the vacuum left by ISIS, it has to revive dormant cells or rebuild influence almost from scratch. So there is an opportunity there to shape the communities in which ISIS operates today.

So the expulsion of the Islamic State offers a rare opportunity, I would say, to implement a strategy to build an alternative to jihadist organizations, more so than you were able in 2014 when dozens of different armed groups operated in these areas.

So the liberation of these areas by the U.S.-led coalition creates a de facto American sphere of influence, which both Russia and the regime have accepted for now, at least. This counterterrorism strategy involves a more foresighted or farsighted policy of establishing de facto safe zones in part of Syria where inhabitants can be protected from jihadists and from the regime and where the international community can also ensure that al-Qaeda, which now operates in only 1 to 2 percent of Syria, at least in a dominant manner, from rolling back into areas from which the Islamic State is expelled or is being expelled.

Those safe zones can be established in the areas where the U.S. and allies have fought ISIS, as I said. The strategy I am proposing is basically a baseline, meaning it requires minimal American commitment. It builds on what the Americans are already doing inside Syria against the Islamic State and without which any fight against jihadism is doomed to fail. So this is the baseline.

The war against the Islamic State has reached the point, in my opinion, where the Americans cannot—or the U.S. forces or the U.S.-led coalition cannot just pull out from Syria, because of, obviously, the ongoing fight against ISIS. It can choose, though—the
U.S. can choose to continue with the current strategy, which I consider disastrous, and allow various forces to fill the ensuing vacuum after ISIS is defeated in some areas.

Instead, I would propose that the U.S. must use its pre-existing leverage to build a sound policy, a sound strategy that breaks away from the current strategy, which overlooks the political environment that enabled the rise of ISIS and other jihadists in the first place.

What is lacking in the current policy is a real kind of strategy that utilizes this leverage to ensure the removal of jihadists, to prevent their return, to protect local communities from indiscriminate bombardments by the Assad regime, and minimize the conflict that is emerging among the various allies in northern Syria, namely the Kurds on one hand and the rebels and Turkey on the other hand.

This strategy, obviously, is not an invitation for an American occupation of Syria or long-term nation-building that President Donald Trump has explicitly criticized. Instead, it is both realistic, essential, and expands on battlefield victories already scored over the past 2½ years in Operation Inherent Resolve against the Islamic State in northern Syria.

The strategy, again, in my opinion, I think should acknowledge the fractured nature of the Syrian conflict today. To get a sense of this fracture, you have to look at kind of the map that Chairman Poe just presented, which basically divides Syria into four quadrants.

One is the caliphate terrain, which extends from eastern Aleppo all the way to Iraq, Iraqi border, all the way to Palmyra in central Syria.

And then you have the second one, the second quadrant, which is rebel-held areas in the north and the south. This is where the Americans and their allies—the Israelis, the Jordanians, and others—have actually done very well in ensuring that jihadists don't have dominance in that area and that there is, like, a relatively reliable moderate rebel coalition there and where al-Qaeda and Islamic State have some presence but they don't dominate.

And the problem there, though, is that the rebel presence there is fragile and requires a policy to ensure that they would withstand the pressure from jihadists. And, actually, today is a good example of that, because Jabhat al-Nusra/al-Qaeda has started to challenge that dynamic in southern Syria.

The third quadrant, very quickly, is the more fragmented northwest——

Mr. POE. The gentleman's time has expired.

[The prepared statement of Mr. Hassan follows:]

Hassan Hassan
Senior Fellow, Tahrir Institute for Middle East Policy
House Committee on Foreign Affairs
02/14/2017 Defeating Terrorism in Syria: A New Way Forward

Stability in Syria is an important national security interest for the United States. Much of Syria is a geographic space controlled or dominated by Al Qaeda and the Islamic State. The country borders key regional partners. The persistent refugee crisis threatens the stability of Europe. The two-pronged threat of international terrorism, emanating from both Al Qaeda and the Islamic State, is fuelled by the continuing conflict.

Despite the grim situation in the country, the US government has an opportunity to stem the challenges presented by the two international terrorist organisations and their enablers.

In fact, Washington has options it did not necessarily have two years ago, including a way to prevent not only the Islamic State but also Al Qaeda and other radical groups from operating in at least 50% to 60% of Syria. These include the territories that the Islamic State controls or once controlled since 2014. Once the Islamic State controls an area, it typically eradicates any Islamist and jihadist cells or support system and disarm the population to prevent local rivalry, which leaves groups like Al Qaeda having to revive dormant cells or rebuilding influence almost from scratch.

So the expulsion of the Islamic State offers a rare opportunity to implement a strategy to build an alternative to jihadist organizations, more so than in 2014 when dozens of different armed groups operated in those areas. The liberation of these areas by the US-led coalition also creates a de facto American sphere of influence, which both Russia and the regime have accepted — at least for the time being.

This counterterrorism strategy involves a more farsighted policy of establishing de facto safe zones in parts of Syria where inhabitants can be protected from the jihadists and the regime, and where the international community can ensure that Al Qaeda does not roll back into the areas from which the Islamic State is expelled. Those safe zones can be established in the areas where the US and its allies fought, or will fight ISIS.

The strategy I am proposing is a baseline. It requires minimal American commitment, building on what the US is already doing in Syria against the Islamic State, without which any fight against jihadism is doomed to fail. Pre-existing resources and hard power should be supplemented with a policy that deliberately immunizes the liberated areas from falling back to extremist forces. This strategy is not an invitation for American occupation or long-term "nation-building" that President Donald Trump has explicitly criticized. Instead, it is both realistic and essential, expanding on battlefield victories already scored over the last two-and-a-half years of Operation Inherent Resolve against the Islamic State in northern, eastern and southern Syria.

The strategy should begin by recognition of the fractured nature of the Syrian conflict today. To get a sense of the situation on the ground, it is important to view it through four quadrants.

The first quadrant is the caliphate terrain. This expanse stretches, albeit not coherently, from As Sukhnah near Palmyra to Albukamal near Iraq, and from there to the Kurdish-controlled Qamashli in the northeastern corner near the Turkish border to Azaz in northwestern Syria. Although the regime still holds pockets in the city of Deir Ezzor, the international coalition has the leverage to dictate how this region should be tackled to prevent the return of ISIS. In this quadrants, three political or military blocs currently focus on fighting ISIS: the Assad regime in Deir Ezzor; the the American-led coalition and the Kurds in Raqqa; and Turkey and its rebel allies in the eastern countryside of Aleppo. If these different forces turn against each other, the consequences could reverse the gains against the Islamic State.

The second quadrant is rebel-held areas in the south, adjacent to the Israeli and Jordanian borders and near Damascus. In stark contrast to northern Syria, relatively quiet fronts exist between the regime and the rebels. Syria's neighbors there, namely Israel and Jordan, have interest in a sustained calm in that region. Regional backers of the opposition that work closely with Jordan, such as Saudi Arabia and the United Arab Emirates, share a similar interest and are committed to preventing extremists from holding sway in that particular region. Both Al Qaeda and the Islamic State have considerable presence in southern Syria, but they are largely contained. The primacy of the rebels and the regime against the jihadists needs to be sustained with a more robust approach to southern Syrian, including by enabling local forces to govern their areas more effectively, building on the existing calm.

The third quadrant is the more fragmented northwest: Idlib, and pockets in rural Aleppo, Hama and Homs. The international community has fewer options in this region because of Al Qaeda's dominance here; unlike the Islamic State, it has integrated into and taken the lead in the mainstream insurgency. Throughout the conflict, Al Qaeda has focused on fighting the Assad regime and rarely sought to impose its own ideology on the local communities in which it operates. As in Yemen and elsewhere, the approach means the fight against Al Qaeda will have to be more sensitive to the local dynamics. This quadrant makes up approximately 2% of Syrian territory, and is the only area where Al Qaeda has relatively dominant presence.

The fourth quadrant is the regime-held areas, roughly 40% of Syria stretching from Deraa in the south to Aleppo in the north.

The US government should approach the Syrian conflict from this compartmentalized outlook. Different areas require different solutions. What works for eastern Syria does not necessarily work for the northwestern corner of Aleppo and Idlib. Similarly, what works for southern Syria does not work for the north. The country is currently fragmented along different conflict dynamics, and therein might exist some solutions.

An approach that recognizes the fragmented nature of the conflict is not the same as division of Syria. Quite the contrary, salvaging different areas in Syria as much as possible helps provide realistic solutions to particular challenges. The US administration can achieve minimally defined objectives of defeating the Islamic State and ensure that the jihadist insurgency cannot physically reconstitute itself again.

In much of Syria, the US has more leverage and presence on the ground than it is publicly recognized. What is lacking is a policy to utilize this leverage to ensure the removal of jihadists, protect local communities from indiscriminate bombardments, and minimize conflict between various allies in northern Syria, namely the Kurds on one hand and the rebels and Turkey on the other.

The US must view southern and eastern Syria, for example, as part of its strategy of fighting extremism in Iraq as well as protecting Jordan and Israel. The focus in these two regions should involve locally accepted governance. The alternative is to hand over these areas to the Assad regime that currently does not have the resources and legitimacy to conquer or hold new areas — such policy will only ensure that the Islamic State will come back, as it did in Palmyra in December despite Russian and Iranian support. Eastern Syria has the added value of its relevance to the stability of Iraq. Even if the US government does not see Syria as important, eastern Syria is inescapably vital for Iraq's border security.

Stabilizing Syria should be a priority for the United States. Reliance on Russia to do the job is a fantasy, and will only perpetuate the conflict and enable jihadists to entrench themselves on the doorsteps of Europe. The areas where the US already has leverage -- from eastern Aleppo along the Turkish border to eastern Syria near the Iraqi border and from there to the Jordanian and Israeli borders – present Washington with a historic opportunity to stabilize the country and ensure an enduring defeat of jihadists.

Mr. POE. And the subcommittee will be in recess for votes. We will start 5 minutes after the last vote has ended. The subcommittee is in recess.

[Recess.]

Mr. POE. The subcommittee will come to order.

Ambassador Hof, we will hear your testimony.

STATEMENT OF THE HONORABLE FREDERIC C. HOF, DIRECTOR, RAFIK HARIRI CENTER FOR THE MIDDLE EAST, ATLANTIC COUNCIL

Ambassador HOF. Thank you, Mr. Chairman.

Mr. Chairman, Ranking Member Keating, members of the committee, I would summarize the key points of my testimony for the record as follows: First, both the Obama and the Trump administrations have defined defeating terror in Syria largely in terms of neutralizing two rival descendants of al-Qaeda in Iraq, namely the so-called Islamic State, ISIL, and the Jabhat Fatah al-Sham, JFS, formerly known as the Nusrah Front.

ISIL has had mainly a live and let live arrangement with the Syrian regime of Bashar al-Assad. JFS has fought the regime while at the same time trying to dominate nationalist Syria First armed rebel units.

Second, terminating the military capabilities of both of these organizations is critically important. But if our goal in Syria is to kill terror and keep it dead, ultimately, a political system reflecting legitimacy has to take hold. Absent a political system that virtually all Syrians see as satisfactory with no superior alternative, absent that, extremists will seek to rise again to fill the vacuum created by gross corruption, incompetence, and brutality.

Third, the main obstacle to political legitimacy in Syria is the survival of a regime headed by Bashar al-Assad and supported by Iran and Russia. The collective punishment and mass homicide survival strategy of this regime has been the main factor behind a humanitarian abomination and a political catastrophe.

Yesterday, the Atlantic Council released a report entitled, "Breaking Aleppo." This report details and documents the campaign of terror inflicted by the Assad regime and Russia on the civilians of Aleppo. It adds to the enormous body of evidence of war crimes and crimes against humanity committed in Syria over the past 6 years, the overwhelming majority of which have been committed by the regime and its allies. These crimes have helped ISIL and JFS enormously in their recruiting.

Fourth, even if the diplomatic pursuit of political legitimacy in Syria is a long-term project, neutralizing ISIL and JFS militarily are urgent priorities. Two successive Presidents have defined both organizations as threats to American national security. ISIL in Syria, which has planned and executed major atrocities in Europe, is currently under attack by a U.S.-led air coalition and a U.S.-advise ground force, largely Kurdish in composition.

I understand the administration is reviewing this military approach in light of Turkish objections to the Kurdish role and the objective desirability of liberating densely populated areas with highly skilled military professionals.

JFS is under attack by U.S. and Russian air assets independently with Syrian nationalist rebel forces seeking ways and means to defeat it. These nationalists will need a tight Russian leash on Assad and on Iranian-led foreign militias in order to move effectively against JFS. It is not yet clear that they will get Russian cooperation.

Fifth and finally, thanks to Russian and Iranian military intervention, Assad seems secure in at least part of Syria. Iran, in particular, needs Assad to bind Syria to Lebanon's Hezbollah, another important Islamist terrorist group. But Assad's political well-being means the indefinite continuation of state terror in Syria.

As the United States and its partners move ideally with dispatch against ISIL and JFS, any temptation to make common cause with or improve the political prospects of Syria's premier practitioner of terror, Bashar al-Assad, must be resisted. Reports of Russian disaffection with Assad and with Iranian-led militias should be explored.

Killing terror in Syria and keeping it dead will, I am afraid, be a long-term endeavor for the United States and its partners, one extending far beyond the defeats of ISIL and JFS.

[The prepared statement of Ambassador Hof follows:]

Ambassador Frederic C. Hof

Director, Rafik Hariri Center for the Middle East, Atlantic Council

House Committee on Foreign Affairs

Subcommittee on Terrorism, Nonproliferation, and Trade

February 14, 2017

"Defeating Terror in Syria: A New Way Forward"

Mr. Chairman, Mr. Ranking Member, Members of the subcommittee: I am honored by your invitation to speak about defeating terror in Syria and pleased to submit this statement for your consideration.

As a one-time military professional I was trained to define a mission and design an accompanying strategy in ways consistent with the desired end-state. In Syria we want terror defeated. We want to kill it and keep it dead. We do not want to neutralize terrorists now only to see them reappear in a few years, as was the case in Iraq. It is the 'keep it dead' part of the desired end-state that makes the battle far more than military in nature. Without an end-state reflecting political legitimacy in Syria – a political system seen by virtually all citizens as satisfactory and with no superior alternative – extremists will seek again to fill a governance vacuum produced by one family's corruption, incompetence, and brutality.

Syria today is a problem from hell. Its internal conflict approaches its sixth year. It is the humanitarian abomination of the 21st century. It has killed hundreds of thousands of people, mainly civilians. Starting with a population of 23 million it has hemorrhaged nearly 5 million refugees and displaced internally over 6 million. More than 13 million require urgent humanitarian aid. Tens of thousands of Syrians have disappeared in government prisons, suffering unspeakable acts of torture, starvation, sexual abuse, and execution. Upwards of one million Syrians have been besieged by their own government, denied the basics of nutrition and medicine. Adding to the misery of Syrian civilians already on the receiving end of state terror is the presence in Syria of two competing terrorist groups: ISIS (ISIL, Islamic State, Daesh) and Jabhat Fatah al-Sham (JFS), rival descendants of Al Qaeda in Iraq (AQI).

Syria is also a political catastrophe. What happens in Syria does not stay in Syria. Refugees have placed great burdens on three countries close to the United States: Turkey, Jordan, and Lebanon. In 2015 one million migrants – most from Syria – made their way in a modern day mass odyssey to western Europe and Scandinavia, roiling the politics of our closest allies. And an emboldened Russia allied itself with Iran's special brand of Islamist extremism to preserve in Syria a client regime subservient to Iran, one totally in the service of Lebanon's Hezbollah. Reacting to the military success of Moscow and Tehran, NATO ally Turkey has joined with Iran and Russia in what it hopes will be a new Syrian peace process that safeguards Turkish interests.

Both the Obama and Trump administrations have defined defeating terror in Syria largely in terms of neutralizing the two rival AQI descendants: ISIS and JFS (the former Nusra Front). Indeed, terminating their military capabilities is critically important. Yet it will not suffice. Not if the desired end-state in Syria involves keeping both groups dead and rendering potentially more lethal successors stillborn.

This is why the Russian-Iranian preservation of the Assad regime presents such a challenge to defeating terror in Syria. Assad has been a poster child for ISIS and JFS recruitment: particularly of foreign fighters. The Independent International Commission of Inquiry into the Syrian Arab Republic, reporting to the UN Human Rights Council, has detailed the horrific war crimes and crimes against humanity committed by the Assad regime, ISIS, JFS, and others: the overwhelming majority by the regime. The reports of the Commission have been substantiated and expanded upon by numerous non-governmental organizations. The United States has facilitated the removal from Syria and safe-keeping of literally tons of evidence of egregious criminal behavior by Assad and his agents.

The point here is neither to catalogue the crimes nor try the perpetrators. Rather, it is simply this: there can be no political legitimacy in Syria and therefore no permanent defeat of terror as long as the Assad extended family and entourage wield political power in any part of the country. Leave aside persuasive evidence of Assad regime complicity in promoting ISIS and other extremists as convenient enemies of choice. Too much blood has been spilled, too many lives ruined, and too few acts of mercy and human decency performed: all because a single family elected to use collective punishment to survive politically. Russia and Iran know this. Assad's apologists know it. Perhaps Assad himself knows it. But some or all of them are content for the regime to continue to rule through state terror. This is not a pathway to legitimacy. This is not a prescription for defeating terror in Syria.

A prerequisite for killing terror in Syria and keeping it dead is for the Assad regime – family, enablers, and entourage – to be replaced by what the June 30, 2012 Geneva Final Communique referred to as a "transitional governing body," one exercising full executive power and reflecting broad national consensus. But Russia and Iran – for separate, though compatible reasons - have purchased for their joint client something that looks like military victory. This leaves the United States stuck with a situation crying out for the rapid military defeat of ISIS and JFS, but no clear way forward to sealing that victory, because a polarizing war criminal remains politically ensconced in Damascus. The best we can do near-term under the circumstances is to defeat militarily these AQI descendants – particularly ISIS – in a way that does not strengthen a regime whose behavior pumps oxygen into the lungs of ISIS and JFS.

There are significant differences between these rival AQI descendants beyond the fact that they despise each other. ISIS has defied Al Qaeda leadership and has declared a 'caliphate' in the territory it seized in Syria and Iraq: territory initially equivalent in size to the United Kingdom. In Syria ISIS has, for the most part, observed a live-and-let live relationship with the regime of Bashar al-Assad. Much of ISIS' military effort in Syria has been focused on nationalist rebels opposing Assad, on JFS, and on Kurds.

JFS, on the other hand, has fought Assad even as it tries to marginalize nationalist rebels and bring the armed anti-Assad uprising under its control. Although it claims to have broken with Al Qaeda, its leaders have demonstrated fealty to Ayman Al-Zawahiri over the years. Whereas ISIS has conducted and inspired acts of terrorism abroad, JFS seems to have restricted its terror activities to Syria, although it stands accused of having hosted Al Qaeda foreigners with transnational terror ambitions.

Notwithstanding important differences between them, both AQI descendants merit early neutralization. And both may require new approaches in order to be beaten thoroughly.

Since September 2014 the United States, with several coalition partners, has been pursuing ISIS in central and eastern Syria with aircraft. After the battle for Kobani later that year, the Kurdish People's Protection Units – the YPG – became the main ground combat component for the anti-ISIS coalition in

Syria. Two-and-one-half years later ISIS remains headquartered in its Syrian 'capital,' Raqqa, after having mounted major terror operations in Paris, Brussels, Istanbul, and Ankara.

The YPG's objective is establish a Syrian Kurdish autonomous zone along the border with Turkey. Given the close relationship between the YPG and the Kurdish Workers' Party (PKK) – an organization designated as terrorist by the United States – Ankara has objected strenuously to the YPG serving as the ground force for the American-led coalition. American special operators advising the YPG in its counter-ISIS operations have attempted to mitigate this objection by training eastern Syrian non-Kurdish forces to work with the YPG under the umbrella of an organization called the Syrian Democratic Forces (SDF). Although the YPG has fought well, neither its interests nor its capabilities make it the ideal force for a block-to-block fight in Arab cities like Raqqa and Deir Ezzor. As I understand it, Arab elements of the SDF would take the lead in entering Raqqa while mainly Kurdish elements would surround the city. One wonders about the level of urban combat expertise resident in the SDF.

The American-led bombing campaign and the work of the SDF on the ground deserve some credit for the gradual shrinkage of ISIS-controlled territory in Syria. Many ISIS leaders and fighters have been killed. Towns and villages important to the logistical link between ISIS in Syria and ISIS in Iraq have been liberated. The nature of ISIS itself – the fact that in Syria it is an imposed entity with significant Iraqi presence in the leadership ranks, the fact that it spends more time fighting opponents of a hated regime than the regime itself, and the fact that its sectarian brutality has inspired widespread resentment – has also contributed to its decline. But this despicable organization has had the time not only to enslave Syrians and perhaps influence young Syrian minds, but to plan in Raqqa significant terrorist operations inflicted on Turkey and western Europe. How much longer will it be permitted to breathe in Syria?

As it reviews anti-ISIS strategy in Syria, the new administration should take a hard look at how and when ISIS will be finished off militarily. Since the ISIS atrocity in Paris in November 2015 I have been advocating that a professional, American-led ground force coalition-of-the-willing replace Kurdish and Arab militiamen to close with and kill ISIS rapidly and with minimal collateral damage. Saudi Arabia, the UAE, and Bahrain have long since volunteered to put forces in Syria to fight ISIS: an offer that drew a strong objection not from the ISIS so-called 'caliph,' but from Assad's foreign minister. Other candidates for the coalition would include Turkey (which already has combat forces in Syria), Jordan, and France.

As an Army veteran who served in Vietnam and Lebanon I am not searching for new opportunities to employ in combat American uniformed personnel already over-committed and over-deployed. On the other hand, two successive Presidents have defined ISIS as a serious threat to American security. We may get lucky and watch the Syrian segment of this organization either preemptively vanish from Raqqa and other populated places or collapse militarily in the face of militiamen barely schooled in the complexities and techniques of fighting in built-up areas. But we cannot count on luck.

Ideally the Pentagon is examining several issues beyond ground force composition. How can ISIS be neutralized in populated areas without adding to the humanitarian catastrophe? What kinds of local administrations will be established in the wake of liberation? How can United Nations relief convoys be expedited? How can civilians in liberated central and eastern Syria be protected from an Assad regime – ISIS' principal enabler in Syria – that has pledged to restore its rule over all of Syria? Perhaps an opportunity will arise in liberating central and eastern Syria from ISIS for the United States and its partners to facilitate the creation of a decent, inclusive government it can recognize and support as an alternative to a regime whose existence is catnip for terrorists.

The near-term military neutralization of Al Qaeda's JFS has challenges distinct from those associated with ISIS. Much of the JFS combat power is centered in the Idlib area of northwestern Syria. Unlike ISIS, JFS has made fighting the Assad regime a high priority. In places like eastern Aleppo it fought alongside nationalist, anti-Assad rebels against the regime and pro-regime Shiite militiamen assembled by Iran: foreign fighters from Lebanon, Iraq, and Afghanistan. JFS also worked hard – as it has for years – to dominate the armed Syrian opposition and to draw recruits from the ranks of other organizations. Many of those groups have concluded that JFS – like ISIS – must be neutralized.

For nationalist rebel forces to confront JFS militarily and resist any temptation to collaborate with it against a common foe, attacks on them by the Assad regime and its Shiite militia supporters must cease. Russia, according to some opposition sources, has shown interest in promoting and monitoring a ceasefire that would facilitate the anti-JFS operations of nationalist rebel forces.

JFS would not be a party to a ceasefire. Indeed, JFS targets have been recently engaged by American combat aviation. But for the nationalist Syrian opposition to confront JFS militarily, Moscow will have to keep a tight leash on Assad and Iran. Even if Moscow truly wants to do so, it will not be easy. In any event, American support for armed, nationalist Syrian opposition units with which Washington has developed relationships over the years should be maintained and enhanced. These units – not undisciplined, looting Iranian-led militias or a depleted Syrian army – will be the ground combat component of any serious effort to neutralize JFS.

In the end, however, defeating terror in Syria will require legitimate governance for Syria. Russia has supported a regime it knows to be illegitimate for two reasons: military operations in Syria have enabled President Putin to tell his domestic audience that Russia has defeated an alleged regime change campaign by the United States and is therefore back as a great power; and he has been able to tell Arab leaders that he stands by his friends, no matter how regrettable their habits. Iran has supported Assad because it knows that he will do whatever Tehran asks of him to support Hezbollah in Lebanon. Hezbollah is Iran's long arm of penetration into the Arab World; it threatens Israel as it holds Lebanon captive. Iran realizes that no other President of Syria would accept a relationship of subordination to it and to Hezbollah's leader, Hassan Nasrallah.

Thanks to Russian and Iranian military intervention Assad seems secure in at least part of Syria for as far as the eye can see. Assad's political well-being means the indefinite continuation of state terror in Syria. As the United States and its partners move – ideally with dispatch – against ISIS and JFS, any temptation to make common cause with or improve the political prospects of Syria's premier practitioner of terror – Bashar al-Assad – must be resisted. Rumors of Russian disaffection with Assad and Iranian-led militias should be explored, though without any expectation of a positive result.

ISIS and JFS can and should be defeated militarily. Terror, however, will be killed in Syria only when legitimate governance, reflecting inclusivity and rule of law, replaces family rule based on collective punishment and mass homicide. So long as the latter prevails responses to it will inevitably include appeals to sectarianism, extremism, and terror. Moscow and Tehran know this quite well. Regrettably they are in charge and they seem not to care. Defeating the descendants of Al Qaeda may produce, in liberated areas, a decent alternative to Assad rule. Still, it is likely that transitioning all of Syria from that rule to terrorist-killing legitimacy will be a long-term national security endeavor for the United States and its partners.

Mr. Poe. Thank you, Ambassador Hof.
Ms. Dalton.

STATEMENT OF MS. MELISSA DALTON, SENIOR FELLOW, CENTER FOR STRATEGIC AND INTERNATIONAL STUDIES

Ms. Dalton. Chairman Poe, Ranking Member Keating, and distinguished members of the subcommittee, it is an honor to testify before you today with my excellent colleagues Ambassador Frederic Hof and Hassan Hassan.

Syria stands today at the epicenter of a regional conflict with global consequences for U.S. interests. Countering terrorism is one aspect of a deeper problem set. The Trump administration and the Congress have the opportunity to change the course of U.S. policy toward Syria by nesting short-term operations into a strategy.

Americans have no interest in perennial military interventions in the Middle East. We have demands for resources at home and competing geostrategic objectives in Europe and Asia. However, the United States has compelling reasons to counter terrorism and to address the broader factors that have enabled the rise of the so-called Islamic State and al-Qaeda's affiliate in Syria, Jabhat Fatah al-Sham. The growth of Iranian proxy groups and a battle-hardened Lebanese Hezbollah in Syria also pose counterterrorism challenges.

Additionally, the United States has to contend with intertwined realities that could challenge its ability to influence outcomes to its advantage. Among these reasons are: Countering terrorists and the roots of terrorism, which threaten the U.S. homeland and our allies and partners; preventing military confrontation with Russia and Iran while limiting the long-term subversive influence they could have in the region; and stemming conflict emanating from Syria from further destabilizing neighboring states in Europe.

Achieving U.S. objectives in Syria will require inherent tradeoffs in the policy choices the Trump administration could pursue. Complicating matters, 6 years of war have torn Syria apart. It no longer exists a unitary whole, requiring different approaches in the north, south, east, and west. Woven throughout the options in Syria are geopolitical choices with which the United States will have to grapple, including how to manage tensions with Russia in a way that secures U.S. interests and contests Russian aggression globally while cooperating where it is advantageous and feasible; how to calibrate pressure on Iran's destabilizing activities without provoking blowback to U.S. Forces operating in the area and while attaining an enduring political outcome in Syria; and how to manage deeply fraught relations with NATO ally Turkey while leveraging the highly capable YPG to fight ISIS in northern Syria.

The Trump administration and Congress should work together to forge a coordinated U.S. strategy for Syria with allies and partners. The goals of this strategy should be to degrade ISIS and JFS, achieve a nationwide cessation of hostilities and a negotiated transition of power in Damascus, and consolidate counterterrorism gains by knitting together local security and governance in the four segments of Syria.

Such an approach will require leveraging multiple tools of U.S. statecraft, including: Registering strong concerns with Russia and

Iran about their support for Assad's brutal tactics and their long-term ambitions in Syria and being prepared to back up those concerns with sanctions and coercion; rebuilding communication and trust with Turkey. While pressing on human rights concerns, we should emphasize the criticality of working through differences as NATO allies. Bolstering support to Iraqi Prime Minister Haider al-Abadi and his efforts to restore security and stability in Iraq. If Iraq falters, ISIS and other terrorist groups will regrow in western Iraq and push back into Syria. Working with the U.N. to leverage and integrate the Astana process into a U.N.-mediated negotia- tions, calibrating sanctions pressure on Putin to convince Assad to accede to the negotiating table, requiring Russian action before al- leviating sanctions. Ukraine should not be a quid pro quo for Syria. Synchronizing operations for Raqqa and Mosul to squeeze ISIS, and aligning covert and noncovert approaches versus ISIS and JFS.

Letting operational conditions on the ground inform strategic ad-justments and withdrawal timelines. Countering ISIS and JFS will be a multiyear effort. Increasing both special operations forces and conventional ground forces in Syria and Iraq, based on com-manders' assessed requirements, conducting training and combat operations with local partners. Consolidating gains from oper-ations, knitting connections among local security forces and govern-ance structures so that terrorist groups cannot grow back. Being strategic about deploying the local partner forces that will be the most credible, accounting for ethno-sectarian differences, even if it requires a slower pace for operations.

If the United States commits resources to establishing a safe zone, I recommend constructing one in southern Syria where oper-ational dynamics are clearer than in the north and to ensure that it ties to political negotiations to end the civil war so as to avoid an open-ended commitment.

We should also enhance intelligence sharing and improved co-ordination among military intelligence and law enforcement enti-ties and continue to provide humanitarian assistance to besieged civilian areas with clear and immediate repercussions in the case of outside interference.

Finally, we should seek a new authorization for the use of force for the U.S. intervention in Syria and Iraq providing for oper-ational flexibility to U.S. commanders. The presence of ISIS and al-Qaeda in Syria demands our immediate attention. However, the United States must anchor its counterterrorism approach in a broader strategy if it is to prevail.

Thank you. I look forward to your questions.

[The prepared statement of Ms. Dalton follows:]

CSIS | CENTER FOR STRATEGIC & INTERNATIONAL STUDIES

Statement before the

House Foreign Affairs Committee

Subcommittee on Terrorism, Nonproliferation, and Trade

"Defeating Terrorism in Syria:
A New Way Forward"

A Testimony by:

Melissa G. Dalton

Senior Fellow and Deputy Director,

International Security Program

Center for Strategic and International Studies (CSIS)

February 14, 2017

2172 Rayburn House Office Building

Chairman Poe, Ranking Member Keating, and distinguished Members of the Subcommittee, it is an honor to testify before you today with my excellent colleagues Ambassador Frederic Hof and Hassan Hassan on options for countering terrorist groups in Syria.

This testimony is informed in part by a scenario-based workshop on Syria conducted in November 2016 at the Center for Strategic and International Studies.

Why Syria Matters

Syria today stands at the epicenter of a regional conflict with global consequences for U.S. interests and objectives. Countering terrorism is one aspect of a deeper problem set. This is a multifaceted conflict destabilizing the Middle East and Europe and raising the possibility of a broader war.

Syria's civil war has raged for six years, beginning as peaceful protests against the brutality of President Bashar al-Assad's regime and descending into a deadly spiral, with over 500,000 thousand killed, millions becoming refugees and internally displaced people (IDPs), and thousands besieged by regime, Russian, Iranian attacks, and non-state actor attacks. It has spawned the greatest human catastrophe since World War II. The United States and members of the international community have struggled to effectively address the crisis in Syria. There truly are no good policy options at this point, as all choices entail significant risks. The U.S. public wants a strong America but does not want to become embroiled in another conflict on the scale of the post–9/11 interventions in Iraq and Afghanistan. However, the current limited approach in Syria – focused primarily on counterterrorism – has been quite financially costly to U.S., allied, and partner interests and arguably has diminished U.S. leadership credibility across the globe. The Trump administration and the Congress have the opportunity to change the course of U.S. policy towards Syria, addressing the terrorist threats emanating from the area by nesting short-term operations into a strategy.

Americans have no interest in perennial military interventions in the Middle East. The United States has demands for resources at home and competing geostrategic objectives in Europe and Asia. However, the United States has compelling reasons to not only counter terrorist groups but also to address the broader factors that have enabled the rise of the so-called Islamic State (ISIS) and al-Qaida's affiliate in Syria, Jabhat Fateh al-Sham (JFS). The growth of Iranian proxy groups and a battle-hardened Lebanese Hezbollah in Syria also pose counter terrorism challenges. Additionally, the United States has to contend with intertwined realities in the Middle East that could challenge its ability to negotiate and influence outcomes to its advantage. Among these reasons are: countering terrorists and the roots of terrorism, which threaten the U.S. homeland and our allies and partners; preventing military confrontation with Russia and Iran while limiting the long-term, subversive influence they could have in the region; and stemming conflict emanating from Syria from further destabilizing neighboring states and Europe.

Achieving U.S. objectives in Syria will require inherent tradeoffs in the policy choices the Trump administration could pursue. It is likely that only some of these goals will be achieved, and possibly at the expense of others. Inherent in resolving the tensions among these interests will be determining the priority afforded to Syria as an issue to tackle within the Trump administration, and how they see its importance relative to other global interests.

Current Operational Dynamics

The grinding Syrian civil war has grown increasingly intense and sectarian, particularly over the past three years. It has pit Syrian government forces and their foreign allies, including Russia and Iran, against a range of antigovernment insurgents. These opposition fighters include ISIS and JFS, as well as a constellation of Syrian Kurdish and Arab rebels, who are supported by the United States, other Arab countries, and Turkey. U.S. and coalition strikes have reduced ISIS and JFS numbers, with ISIS now numbering between 19,000 and 25,000 foot soldiers and JFS between 5,000 and 10,000.[1] The United States reportedly has 500 special operations forces in Syria and has conducted over 2,700 air strikes since May 2016 with anti-ISIS coalition members.[2]

Based upon data released by Russia's Central Election Commission there are approximately 4,000 to 5,000 Russian troops thought to be in Syria. However, this does not include Russian special forces and other similar personnel, which would increase this estimate.[3] Russia's intervention in 2015 has since enabled the Syrian government to reinforce its positions, retake territory from Syrian rebels, and regain Aleppo, using brutal tactics against Syrian civilians and civilian targets including hospitals and schools. Assad's Syrian Army currently fields between 80,000 and 100,000 troops.[4] Further buttressing Assad's forces, Iran has mobilized between 115,000 and 128,000 fighters in Syria, comprised of Lebanese Hezbollah and Syrian, Iraqi, Afghan, and Pakistani recruits.[5] Taken together, there is a significant fighting force with active supply lines from external allies backing Assad.

The Syrian Democratic Forces (SDF), supported by the U.S.-led coalition and comprising mostly of Syrian Kurdish and some Sunni Arab groups, number approximately 35,000 to 50,000 soldiers.[6] They successfully pushed ISIS out of areas in northern Syria in 2016. Substantial governance and security challenges, however, remain in the recovered areas. For one, Turkey's intervention in northern Syria, *Operation Euphrates Shield,*[7] has complicated U.S. and partnered security efforts,

---

[1] Schmitt, Eric. "Al Qaeda Turns to Syria, with a Plan to Challenge ISIS." *The New York Times.* May 15, 2016. https://www.nytimes.com/2016/05/16/world/middleeast/al-qaeda-turns-to-syria-with-a-plan-to-challenge-isis.html.

[2] Munoz, Carlo. "Pentagon sends hundreds more U.S. special operations forces into Syria." *The Washington Times.* December 10, 2016, http://www.washingtontimes.com/news/2016/dec/10/pentagon-sends-hundreds-more-us-special-operations/; U.S. Department of Defense. "Operation Inherent Resolve." February 8, 2017. https://www.defense.gov/News/Special-Reports/0814_Inherent-Resolve.

[3] "Commission Inadvertently Reveals Russian Troop Numbers in Syria." *The Moscow Times.* September 22. 2016, https://themoscowtimes.com/news/duma-voting-figures-reveal-over-4000-russian-troops-in-syria-55439.

[4] Al-Ma Sri, Abdulrahman. "Analysis: The Fifth Corps and the State of the Syrian Army." *Atlantic Council.* January 13, 2017, http://www.atlanticcouncil.org/blogs/syriasource/analysis-the-fifth-corps-and-the-state-of-the-syrian-army

[5] Raided, Majid. "Iran's Forces Outnumber Assad's in Syria." *Gatestone Institute.* November 24, 2016, https://www.gatestoneinstitute.org/9406/iran-soldiers-syria.

[6] CSIS Syria Stabilization Workshop, November 2016.

[7] In August 2016, Turkey launched "Euphrates Shield" seeking to both secure its territory from ISIS and halt the advance of the YPG militia. In approaching the city of al-Bab, the advance slowed as ISIS increasing relied on subterranean and tunnel warfare, suicide vehicle-borne improvised explosive devices, and man-portable anti-tank guided missiles. Notably, in the face of these emerging challenges, the Turkish military altered its force composition in the Operation Euphrates Shield and started deploying more commando units to support local Syrian forces. "ISIL fighters 'besieged' in Syria's al-Bab in Aleppo." *Al Jazeera.* February 6, 2016, http://www.aljazeera.com/news/2017/02/isil-fighters-besieged-syria-al-bab-aleppo-170206172706993.html. Kasapoglu, Can. "Operation Euphrates Shield: Progress and scope." *Al Jazeera.* February 3, 2017,

as U.S. and Turkish objectives clash regarding the role and reach of Syrian Kurdish forces. Turkey bitterly opposes the role and territorial control of the Syrian Kurdish People's Protection Units (YPG) that have linkages to the Kurdistan's Workers Party (PKK), which Turkey deems a terrorist organization. Additionally, Arab-Kurd tensions in northern Syria, increasing as the SDF YPG units press into Arab communities, present a specter of a civil war to come.

The northern Syrian city of al-Bab presents a stark picture of how competing forces in Syria will either have to cooperate or risk confrontation in the combined fight against ISIS. ISIS controls al-Bab, its last stronghold west of Raqqa. Syrian government forces, backed by Russia, are advancing on the city in parallel with Turkish-supported Syrian opposition groups to root out ISIS. The fight in al-Bab will be a test of the newly-brokered Russian-Turkish cooperation in Syria, and whether Syrian forces on both sides will abide by that agreement to address a common enemy or turn on each other.[8]

<u>Fragmented Territorial Control</u>

Syria no longer exists as a unitary whole, as the civil war has cleaved it into at least four parts. Assad's forces, backed by Russia, Iran, and Lebanese Hezbollah, control the western segment, a strategic corridor from Damascus to Aleppo providing access to the Mediterranean and the Assad family's Alawite community in Latakia, and enabling Iranian resupply and command and control to Lebanese Hezbollah. In the second segment, Sunni Arab tribes occupy the desert connecting eastern Syria and western Iraq, disenfranchised by Assad's crackdown and the post-Saddam era of repression in Iraq, wherein ISIS easily implanted its so-called caliphate. In the third segment, Syria's northwest is comprised of a marbled blend of opposition groups supported by Turkey, the United States, and the Gulf states, and into which JFS has secured safe haven. By negotiating and cooperating with other opposition groups in northern Syria, and with perceptions of U.S. withdrawal pervasive among Syrian opposition members, JFS has demonstrated an ability to adapt to changing conditions and its influence has grown among opposition groups.[9] U.S.-backed groups have grown weaker. Aside from being one of the most powerful groups in Syria, JFS' ability to adapt could contribute to its longevity.[10] The Islamist group Ahrar al-Sham receives substantial support from Turkey and has also recently attracted a number of opposition groups to its ranks.[11] Syria's fourth segment, in the south surrounding Deraa, is closely watched by Israel and Jordan, along with Syria opposition groups supported by Gulf partners. Relative to the four other segments, clashes between regime and opposition forces occur less frequently there.

According to the Pentagon, ISIS has lost 43 percent of its total caliphate, including 57 percent of its territory in Iraq and 27 percent of its territory in Syria.[12] While it could retain some territory,

http://www.aljazeera.com/indepth/opinion/2017/02/operation-euphrates-shield-progress-scope-170201133525121.html.

[8] Anne Barnard, "Battle to Retake Syrian City Turns into a Geopolitical Test of the War, *The New York Times,* February 8, 2017, https://www.nytimes.com/2017/02/08/world/middleeast/battle-al-bab-syria-geopolitical-test.html
[9] "The Jihadi Threat: ISIS, Al Qaeda, and Beyond." *United States Institute of Peace*, p. 12. December 2016, http://www.usip.org/sites/default/files/The-Jihadi-Threat-ISIS-Al-Qaeda-and-Beyond.pdf.
[10] Ibid., 24.
[11] Aaron Lund, "The Jihadi Spiral," Diwan, (Carnegie Endowment for International Peace), February 8, 2017, http://carnegie-mec.org/diwan/67911
[12] "The Jihadi Threat: ISIS, Al Qaeda, and Beyond," 24.

its capabilities have been markedly degraded.[13] Even still, ISIS remains a resilient force. Without the ability to counter the airpower of the U.S.-led coalition, ISIS fighters continually demonstrate discipline and a willingness to fight.[14] ISIS is also expanding its global reach to affiliates and individuals through remote plotting and virtual links. As a result, ISIS commanders in Syria and Iraq are able to not only inspire but also direct operations globally.[15] ISIS has also taken advantage of the migrant exodus and political climate in Europe to spread its influence and operatives and sow fear. With the idea of ISIS still alive and well, it is possible for it to easily regrow in Sunni areas of Syria and Iraq, if local community actors do not consolidate security and governance gains in those areas.

Current Diplomatic Efforts

After pledging to strengthen a fragile ceasefire in Syria,[16] representatives from Russia, Turkey and Iran recently discussed details of implementing the Syrian ceasefire agreement in Astana, Kazakhstan.[17] Russia and Iran are split over the possible future participation of the United States: while Russia seems open to the idea of U.S. involvement, Iran opposes any such notion.[18] Blaming Iranian-backed Shia militias for violating the fragile ceasefire agreement by launching assaults against rebel-held areas, the Syrian opposition has objected to Iran's role in Astana.[19] United Nations leadership is hopeful that the meetings in Astana will bolster the UN-sponsored intra-Syria talks, which are guided by UN Security Council resolution 2254 (2015).[20] According to Russian Foreign Minister Sergey Lavrov, Astana is not meant to replace the UN format.[21]

Policy Choices

The Trump administration will choose a Syria policy from a range of known options, most of which are not mutually exclusive and several of which have been attempted at least in part by the Obama administration. All options in Syria entail risks and tradeoffs—including choices of inaction or tacit acceptance of the status quo. This requires the Trump administration to determine what is most important to U.S. short- and long-term interests, including on countering terrorism.

Woven throughout these Syria-specific options are geopolitical choices with which the Trump administration and Congress will have to grapple, including:

---

[13] Ibid., 13.

[14] Ibid.

[15] Bridget Moreng. "ISIS' Virtual Puppeteers," Foreign Affairs. September 21. 2016.
https://www.foreignaffairs.com/articles/2016-09-21/isis-virtual-puppeteers; Rukmini Callimachi, "Not 'Lone Wolves' After All: How ISIS Guides World's Terror Plots From Afar," The New York Times, February 4, 2017, https://www.nytimes.com/2017/02/04/world/asia/isis-messaging-app-terror-plot.html?_r=0

[16] Tahhan. Zena and Dylan Collins. "Astana summit: Opposition sets demands for new talks." *Al Jazeera.* January 24, 2017, http://www.aljazeera.com/news/2017/01/astana-summit-opposition-sets-demands-talks-170124163538146.html.

[17] "Russia, Turkey, Iran discuss Syria ceasefire in Astana." *Al Jazeera.* February 6, 2017, http://www.aljazeera.com/news/2017/02/russia-turkey-iran-syria-ceasefire-astana-170206080423207.html.

[18] Ibid.

[19] Ibid.

[20] "Syria: UN, Security Council welcome Astana talks and look forward to intra-Syrian negotiations." *UN News Centre.* February 1, 2017, http://www.un.org/apps/news/story.asp?NewsID=56086#.WJzAAIUrLcs.

[21] "Russia, Turkey, Iran discuss Syria ceasefire in Astana."

- How to manage tensions with Russia in a way that secures U.S. interests and contests Russian aggression globally while cooperating where it is advantageous and feasible[22];

- How to calibrate pressure on Iran's destabilizing activities without provoking blowback to U.S. forces operating in Syria and Iraq, and while attaining an enduring political outcome in Syria[23]; and

- How to manage deeply fraught relations with NATO ally Turkey while leveraging the operationally-capable YPG to fight ISIS in northern Syria.

The major policy options are:

1) Allow Russia and Iran to back Assad in consolidating control of western Syria. This could be an intentional policy choice or simply the outcome of events on the ground continuing on their current course. If the Trump administration drags its heels on deciding on Syria, this may well be the result regardless of intent. Having secured Aleppo, Assad's forces, backed by Russia and Iran, are pounding Idlib, where JFS and other opposition groups have embedded among civilians, and are seeking to remove ISIS from al-Bab with Turkey's cooperation. Under this option, the United States could abandon its insistence that Assad must go and make a deal with the Russians to ensure continued counterterrorism efforts against ISIS and JFS. Washington could also reduce support to local Syrian rebels in order to deescalate tensions with Russia, Assad, and Turkey. The United States could still maintain support for international humanitarian operations in Syria, the neighboring region, and in Europe, but Washington would cease to try to curb Assad's or Russian targeting of civilian populations.

The risks to this approach begin inside Syria. A deep-seated Sunni insurgency would likely continue to challenge Assad throughout much of the country, providing fertile ground for terrorist recruitment and providing safe haven for terrorist groups. Even if the United States stands down on its efforts to train and equip resistance groups, regional partners may still support local Syrian groups to combat Assad and Iranian influence. Refugee and IDP flows will worsen with Assad's consolidation, putting additional pressure on Lebanon, Jordan, Turkey, Iraq, and Europe. A Russian- and Iranian-protected Assad enclave in the Middle East, ringed by Iranian-backed militias, could serve as a beachhead for attacks against Israel, Turkey, and other allies, or even U.S. interests at points in the not-so-distant future. It is also unclear whether Russia would be satisfied with this foothold in the Middle East or if it would harbor grander ambitions to reclaim all of Syria or even to look beyond its borders. Beyond Syria, U.S. strategic and moral credibility and resolve would be questioned if we were to walk away from a long-standing policy to contest Assad, even if it were to come with a change of administration. Certainly, America's moral suasion would suffer.

2) Strengthen the counterterrorism approach to "defeat" ISIS and al-Qaida. President Trump has made it clear that he wants to more robustly counter ISIS. A strengthened counterterrorism

---

[22] CSIS will be publishing a report in spring 2017 on a new U.S. Strategy for Russia, a study effort led by Lisa Samp and Dr. Kathleen Hicks.

[23] CSIS will be publishing a report in March 2017, Deterring Iran After the Nuclear Deal, a study effort led by Melissa Dalton and Dr. Kathleen Hicks.

approach would likely include targeting JFS, enhancing intelligence collection, reinforcing U.S. and regional strategic forces presence and force enablers in Syria, and increasing air strikes on ISIS and JFS targets. A counterterrorism policy "on steroids" could also tie together the campaigns against ISIS in Raqqa, Syria, and in Mosul, Iraq, to more effectively squeeze ISIS with greater operational synchronization. The United States might choose to cooperate with Russia and Assad (and thus also Iran) to degrade ISIS and JFS, as these countries might provide ground forces and intelligence. It is critical that both overt and covert operational lines of effort be synchronized to avoid inadvertent conflict or duplication among local partners.

This approach may reduce immediate terrorist threats and accomplish a major policy goal of the administration. The downside, however, is that it does not address underlying challenges or grievances that are rooted in the political, economic, identity, and social dynamics that produce terrorists. In other words, for every terrorist the United States captures or kills, three could take their place, particularly if there is no attempt to hold territory or invest in a political solution or improved governance. Moreover, it is highly unlikely that the United States and its partners will truly "defeat" ISIS, given that it is embedded in a Sunni insurgency in Syria and Iraq. Rather, the United States can degrade ISIS' capabilities and reach to threaten the U.S. homeland and its allies and partners. Still, such a policy would undoubtedly worsen humanitarian conditions, as it would give Assad, backed by Russia and Iran, license to indiscriminately target civilians with impunity under the guise of countering terrorism. The United States would be seen as complicit in these activities and as a partner to Assad, Russia, and Iran, further inflaming longer-term Sunni terrorist movements against the West. As such, it would risk significant blowback from regional Arab partners on other priorities such as Israeli and Gulf security and efforts to pressure Iran. This approach also fails to contain spillover effects, including the possibility that the conflict moves across borders, extremist group exfiltration, and refugee flows into neighboring countries and Europe.

3) Conduct a larger-scale military intervention to pressure Assad. This choice involves the greatest departure from the status quo and would require heavy resourcing and commitment and should require a vote of affirmation from Congress. A U.S. intervention could take the form of implementing no-fly zones, safe zones, enhanced support for Syrian rebels, and/or coercive measures and direct strikes on Assad regime targets. Almost all of these types of interventions require a larger ground force commitment to enforce a change in the military balance, pressure Assad, and create a safe area for humanitarian response efforts. On the high end of ground force requirements under these options, up to 30,000 ground forces could be required to secure a safe zone. This number would include local Syrian, regional, and U.S. and Coalition troops.

The major downside to pursuing this option is that it heightens the potential for miscalculation or escalation with Russia and Iran. Turkey is also likely to resist an intervention if the United States relies upon Syrian Kurdish forces to secure areas, which we undoubtedly would. Syrian rebels with ISIS or JFS sympathies could infiltrate safe zones and conduct attacks or gather intelligence for ISIS and JFS. As Afghanistan and Iraq have demonstrated, large concentrations of U.S. troops can never be perfectly secured. U.S. and coalition ground troops would be magnets for terrorist attacks and a beacon for terrorist recruitment. Such a policy would involve high upfront risks to U.S. and international security and resourcing costs but could accrue gains in local Syrian governance and security over time if part of a greater political strategy for Syria and the region. If the military requirements of the intervention are such that the involvement of U.S. ground troops becomes necessary—a likely reality—then the near-term risk to American lives and treasure could be great.

4) Pursue a negotiated political outcome. President Trump has expressed openness to dealing with Russia but appears to want a hardline tack versus Iran. On Syria, it will be difficult to pursue both goals. Iran will need to be on board with any diplomatic deal involving Syria if such a deal is to endure. It is unlikely that the Russians hold enough leverage over Iran to compel cooperation or that Iran will necessarily see the removal of Assad as in its interests. Washington will likely need to adopt a range of approaches, including carrots and sticks, to persuade Russia and Iran to come to the table on U.S. terms – or to enter the existing Astana process. It is unclear exactly what the right mix of inducements and pressure will be, but it likely will require a more extensive coalition of allies and partners. For example, the United States and Europe could convince Russia to pressure Assad to accede to an agreement and even leave the country in exchange for sanctions relief for Russia – requiring Russia to take the first step before unwinding sanctions, as has been done with sanctions on Iran. A quid pro quo of Syria for Crimea is not only strategically damaging for the United States; it is not necessary. In fact, increasing pressure through secondary sanctions on Russia to persuade Vladimir Putin to make the case to Assad to depart could resonate more deeply – Russia responds more readily to strength.[24] If convinced, Russia could apply both overt and covert pressure on Assad himself and his inner circle, including enhancing financial pressure, information and cyber operations.

There is certainly no guarantee that the Russians would accept such a course or in accepting would abide by their commitments. Further steps might include permitting a sustained Russian military presence in Syria and in the Eastern Mediterranean. Iran will want a pliable replacement to Assad to preserve its influence and access, including Hezbollah's supply and operational reach in the Levant. It is no guarantee that Assad's replacement under such conditions would necessarily yield better results vis-à-vis U.S. interests. The phasing of the negotiations might include starting with creating "no bomb zones," and instituting a true cessation of hostilities. Negotiations should include Syrian opposition leaders, so that Syrians own the solution and the negotiated outcome is more likely to endure.

This is by far the hardest outcome to achieve, as it must have both multilateral and local buy-in for it to endure, and parties to the conflict have competing agendas and interests. It is likely the only option that will deescalate the overall violence in Syria quickly, but very well could require escalation against Russia, Assad, and Iran to achieve it. This is perhaps a U.S. form of the Russian doctrine of "escalate to deescalate," and will require a very nuanced approach to avoid miscalculation. Moreover, absent a shift in the local balance of power, the United States would enter such negotiations with limited leverage, as Secretary John Kerry's negotiations demonstrated. Perhaps the Trump administration can generate its own leverage. Even if it is successful, the United States would be complicit in the actions of Russia, Iran, and the Assad regime against the Syrian people, a high cost to pay to U.S. credibility, and especially if the deal leaves Assad in power.

---

[24] See forthcoming Hicks and Samp CSIS Russia Report in Spring 2017.

Recommendations

The Trump Administration and Congress should work together to forge a coordinated U.S. strategy for Syria with allies and partners, countering terrorism, its underpinnings, and its enablers. The goals of this strategy should be to degrade ISIS and JFS, achieve a nationwide cessation of hostilities and a negotiated transition of power in Damascus, and consolidate security gains by knitting together local security, governance, and development in the four segments of Syria. Such an approach will require leveraging multiple tools of U.S. statecraft, including:

<u>Diplomatic Initiatives</u>

- Registering strong concerns with Russia and Iran about their support for Assad's brutal tactics and their long-term ambitions in Syria (e.g., long-term presence of IRGC-backed groups in Syria) and being prepared to back up those concerns with economic sanctions and military coercion;

- Rebuilding communication and trust with Turkey through Departments of Defense and State and intelligence community contacts;

    o While pressing Turkey on human rights concerns, emphasize the criticality of working through differences as NATO allies.

- Bolstering support to Iraqi Prime Minister Haider al-Abadi and his efforts to restore security and stability in Iraq. If Iraq falters, ISIS and other terrorist groups will regrow in western Iraq and push back into Syria;

- Working with the UN to leverage and integrate the Astana process into UN-mediated negotiations;

- Creating a U.S.-led multilateral forum in which tensions and conflicting objectives can be addressed with key allies and partners on the Syria problem set (including Turkey, Israel, Jordan, and Gulf partners);

- Continuing to work with the international community to provide emergency humanitarian assistance to besieged civilian areas in Syria, with clear and immediate repercussions in the case of outside interference;

    o Beyond the compelling moral imperative to do so, generations of Syrians will remember potential U.S. inaction, which could feed extremist anti-U.S. narratives and boost terrorist recruitment.

<u>Economic Measures</u>

- Calibrating sanctions pressure on Putin to convince Assad to accede to the negotiating table, requiring Russian action before alleviating sanctions and leveraging European secondary sanctions on Russia. Ukraine should not be a quid pro quo for Syria;

- Extracting positive lessons learned from the U.S. and European negotiating experience with Iran to created needed pressure on Russia and Assad for a negotiated political solution;

- Sustaining support to multilateral and USAID initiatives to address humanitarian and community resilience needs in order to consolidate governance gains as ISIS and JFS are pushed out of areas.

Military Operations

- Strengthening coherence of operational planning and efforts across Syria and Iraq, synchronizing operations for Raqqa and Mosul to squeeze ISIS, and aligning covert and non-covert approaches versus ISIS and JFS;

- Letting operational conditions on the ground inform strategic adjustments and withdrawal timelines. ISIS and JFS will not be defeated in the next year; it will require a multi-year effort;

- Increasing both special operations forces and conventional ground forces in Syria and Iraq, based on commanders' assessed requirements, with U.S. conventional forces providing support to U.S. SOF conducting training and combat operations with local partners;

- Enhancing focus on consolidating gains from ground and air operations, setting the conditions now for what comes after ISIS and JFS. Amplify support to and knit connections among local security forces and governance structures in both Syria and Iraq, so that terrorist groups cannot grow back.

- Being strategic about deploying the local partner forces that will be the most credible in providing security to specific communities in the short and long term, accounting for ethno-sectarian differences, even if it requires a slower pace for operations;

  o The blowback effects of Arab-Kurd conflict in northern Syria could be severe if local security forces are mismatched with civilian communities and set the conditions for terrorist exploitation.

- If establishing a safe zone, construct one in southern Syria, where operational dynamics are clearer than in the north;

  o Ensure that the safe zone operation ties to political negotiations to end the civil war so as to avoid an open-ended commitment.

Intelligence Operations

- Enhancing intelligence-sharing and combined operations within the region and with European and regional allies and partners to disrupt terrorist attacks, improving coordination among military, intelligence, and law enforcement entities;

o Combine intelligence sharing across allied and partner ISR platforms to reduce burden on U.S. assets.

<u>Legal Measures</u>

- Seeking a new Authorization for the Use of Force (AUMF) for the U.S. intervention in Syria (and Iraq), providing for operational flexibility to U.S. commanders.

Mr. Poe. I thank all of you all for your testimony. I will recognize myself for 5 minutes.

First of all, I gave each of you a list of the participants as I know them as of today. Ambassador Hof, I will just ask you quickly, is this a fair statement of the lineup of the players?

Ambassador Hof. I think, broadly speaking, Mr. Chairman, it is a fair lineup. The only—the only thing off the top of my head I might take issue with here is listing ISIS under the roster of anti-Assad forces. There has been, for the past 3 years, a live and let live relationship between the regime and ISIS. The regime's military effort, the military effort of Russia has been directed at elements other than ISIS with rare exception.

Mr. Poe. Okay. Thank you. And it is a fair statement that there is an ebb and flow of the anti-Assad forces as to who they are today, whether they are anti-Assad or whether they are just working for their own self-interest in particular areas of the country. Is that a fair statement?

Ambassador Hof. Yes, it is, Mr. Chairman. There is probably an example of just about everything in Syria today.

Mr. Poe. You have the bona fide rebel forces who want to overthrow Assad; you have out-of-towners who are criminals that are looking to loot, pillage the area; you have people coming in to take over territory. You just have everybody there in the anti-Assad group. Is that a fair statement?

Ambassador Hof. You have got local elements that, for criminal purposes, have taken full advantage of local situations. You also—you also have an ebb and flow of people depending on resource availability.

One of the great successes of the al-Qaeda elements in Syria is that they have been pretty well resourced and have been able to pull away young Syrian men who are anti-Assad, originally lined up with the Free Syrian Army and so forth, but who have gone to work for an organization where they know—where breakfast is going to come from, they know they have got a serviceable weapon, they know they have got plenty of ammunition, so that has been a factor as well.

Mr. Poe. Are any of the Middle Eastern countries, Saudi Arabia, Qatar, UAE, are they funding any of these groups like al-Qaeda, quasi-terrorist groups?

Ambassador Hof. I think, Mr. Chairman, the bulk of the evidence suggests that at an official level, no. These governments are not funding al-Qaeda or ISIS or any of those.

Mr. Poe. But it would be a fair statement that money is coming from those countries?

Ambassador Hof. You bet, you bet. It would be a totally fair statement. There is money coming, I think in recent reports, Qatar and Kuwait have earned honorable or dishonorable mentions in this regard.

Mr. Poe. Dishonorable mentions. So you have at least three terrorist groups. You have ISIS, you have al-Qaeda, and you have Hezbollah, three terrorist groups, questionable whose side they are on on any given day.

Let me ask you this. The U.S.—let's talk about the United States' role. In the past, we decided we would fund 5,000 so-called moderate rebels. That turned out to be a disaster. It cost us $½ billion. Armed 60 of them and they surrendered after the first day. I say that to say it is difficult to know who we are dealing with as a country when we turn over American equipment and American money.

What should the United States do? Should we just stay the course, give a little money, a little weapon here and there? Should we go all in with the, you know, with the B-52s? So I say that, not facetiously, but all in all should we just say this is not our battle? Which of those three options, and I am going to ask each of you to give me which option the United States should take from this point on.

Mr. Hassan, which position should the U.S. take?

Mr. HASSAN. I think what the U.S. should be doing and what should——

Mr. POE. Which of those three options?

Mr. HASSAN. I think they have to be more—they have to go all—politically all in, and I think that is where the U.S. has been lagging behind. They haven't pegged a political track to the military track as necessary.

Mr. POE. All right. Ambassador Hof.

Ambassador HOF. I would say all in using a whole-of-government approach to this. It is not entirely a military issue. Against ISIL it is, for sure, but there are—you know, the security of Americans is what is at stake and what is——

Mr. POE. Sure, political solution.

Ambassador HOF [continuing]. Bubbling up out of Syria.

Mr. POE. And Ms. Dalton.

Ms. DALTON. I think we have to go in with a multifaceted approach that pushes hard politically, that creates leverage with Russia and Iran to pressure Assad to come to the negotiating table, and to change the military balance on the ground by continuing to support the groups that we have been working with.

Mr. POE. I thank all three of you.

And I recognize the gentleman from Massachusetts, ranking member, Mr. Keating.

Mr. KEATING. Thank you, Mr. Chairman.

Ms. Dalton, you mentioned in your opening remarks, "Ukraine should not be a quid pro quo for Syria." What prompted those statements from you?

Ms. DALTON. Thank you, Ranking Member Keating. There have been reports of late that as the new administration is examining the policy options before it, which are, of course, global in scale given where the United States sits in the world, that they might take a different approach to Russia and that perhaps there is some transactional trade space to be had in areas where Russia and the United States are conflicting or have been conflicting. And there is a notion that perhaps an agreement could be reached with the Russians such that the United States would turn a blind eye to Russia's activities in Ukraine in Crimea in exchange for Russian cooperation against ISIS in Syria and working with Assad.

The reality is that that would be strategically foolhardy for the United States, in my opinion, to go down that pathway. Russia responds to strength, and rewarding Russia for bad behavior by en-

couraging more bad behavior doesn't seem to be a recipe for success.

Mr. KEATING. Let me follow that up, if I could.

Ms. DALTON. Yeah.

Mr. KEATING. The Trump administration has repeatedly em-
braced the idea that the U.S. should cooperate with Russia on
counter-ISIS or ISIL operations in Syria. How possible is that en-
gagement in security in cooperating with Russia without working
with Iran and its affiliates? Any of you.

Ms. DALTON. Yes. I think—before turning to the Iran bit of that
question, I think it is important to note that the vast majority, up
to 80 percent of Russia's air strikes in Syria have not been on ISIS
targets. They have been on other Syrian opposition groups, some
of which have been supported by the United States and our partners, and against civilian targets in Syria. So the idea—in a very
sort of objective way of looking at this, our objectives are not
aligned with Russia in terms of——

Mr. KEATING. Professor Hof, same question.

Ambassador HOF. Yes, sir. I would certainly not begrudge the administration the ability to conduct its due diligence about the possibility of some kind of diplomatic and even, eventually, military cooperation with Russia. I have—I have my doubts as to whether
there is any there there, but doing the diplomatic due diligence,
look, there is no doubt whatsoever that the leadership in Russia
has no affection, much less respect for Bashar al-Assad. Bashar al-
Assad has served a political purpose, to date, for President Putin.
For our Government to explore whether there is a possibility of
Russia using some leverage to push Assad into meaningful negotiations, I think it is worth a try.

Mr. KEATING. Yeah. Mr. Hassan, how—could you—Mr. Hassan,
I mean, could you follow up, but also talk about the ability of the
U.S. and Russia sharing information, vital information in that
quest.

Mr. HASSAN. Absolutely. I think it is possible to cleave away Russia from Iran but only under one condition, which is that the U.S.
pursues the right policy inside Syria, regardless of how Russia per-
ceives that, which is basically a change in Syria that has seen legitimate—like as a legitimate change inside Syria, and the defeat—
and focus on the political environment inside Syria as much as the
military challenge that ISIS and al-Qaeda pose.

Only then would Russia start to maybe work with Americans in
the right way against the interest of Iran. We know that the priorities of the two countries are different. They are long-term priorities at least.

Mr. KEATING. Perhaps, if I could interrupt just to put this on the
table, we are running out of time, but I think other people will follow up. I haven't heard you talk about safe zones. If you could comment on some of the drawbacks of safe—and dangers of safe zones,
what we should be looking out for, what is possible.

Ambassador HOF. I think the main—the main thing to try to understand about safe zones is that it requires very strong protection
not only from 30,000 feet, not just a no-fly zone, it requires decisive
military power on the ground. This is what distinguishes a safe
zone from a killing zone where people are inadvertently drawn in

to a situation where they are not protected on the ground and as a result, slaughter takes place.

Mr. KEATING. Yeah. And infiltration from terrorists.

I yield back.

Mr. POE. I thank the gentleman.

The Chair recognizes the gentleman from California, Mr. Cook.

Mr. COOK. Thank you very much.

One of the countries that is not listed right on this list or your list is Israel, and a lot of the foreign policy that we have in the United States is very sensitive to Israel's position.

Do you have any comments in regards to how Israel views this situation? I know the relations with Russia isn't bad, but their position against Hezbollah and Iran, I think, is well known, and they consider them a, you know, a major threat to the country. Anyone?

Ms. DALTON. Thank you, Congressman. I believe that, from a security perspective, Israel is very concerned about the growth and development of IRGC-backed groups, not just Lebanese Hezbollah but the up to 115,000 Iranian-backed groups that are present in Syria and bolstering the Assad regime, and what that portends for the long-term presence of those groups in Syria and how that could potentially serve as a beachhead for IRGC activities that could threaten Israel and its interest.

On top of that, the fact that Lebanese Hezbollah has acquired further operational refinement and capability development through its activities in Syria that could then be taken back to Lebanon and threaten Israel, I think is also something that the Israelis are very concerned about from a security perspective.

Mr. COOK. I noticed Hamas was not listed on there. Do you have any comments about Hamas? Anybody? No? They are a nonplayer?

Ambassador HOF. I think, Congressman, Hamas has been essentially a nonplayer in Syria for—there used to be an office in Damascus. It left, and I believe it has been a nonplayer for awhile in the Syrian context.

Mr. COOK. Okay. Going back to Assad. I still—being a history major, and the history of Hezbollah and in Iran and their conduct there, it is very hard for me to accept the Russian position in Syria and some of the other countries there. The pro-Assad forces, I think they are very accurate there. Pro-Assad, obviously Iran, North Korea, China, and Hezbollah. And so I am still very, very nervous about any Russian affiliation with Assad and because of his conduct, both the present ruler and his father, which has been going on for years, and the number of people that have been killed in that country.

I yield back. Thank you.

Mr. POE. The Chair recognizes the gentlelady from Nevada, Ms. Titus.

Ms. TITUS. Thank you, Mr. Chairman.

I would just like to ask you about the perception of the United States in the region within Syria. You know, with the travel ban, with our unwillingness to do our part to help refugees, the recent announcement, perhaps, that they are going to continue to go down this path, what kind of perception will we have to overcome to be successful in the area? And is this working in the hands of some

of the terrorist groups to use as propaganda against us in making
the situation worse? Anybody, or all of you?

Mr. HASSAN. Sure. I think many people, especially people who
are in charge of the campaign against ISIS and al-Qaeda, recognize
that the framing of the fight against these organizations is as important as the military challenge. So if your—if you have like 60
countries fighting ISIS and ISIS is telling everyone that these are
crusaders, these are not fighting us because we are terrorists but
fighting the Sunnis, look at the devastation in Mosul but also look
at the devastation at Aleppo. These are two separate powers doing
work in two countries against Sunnis.

So I think the framing of the fight against ISIS is as crucial as
the military challenge. The ban itself is not as much discussed in
the region as here, obviously, but I think there is a—perception
matters a lot in Syria and Iraq. And that is why there is a danger
in working with the Russians without really working out the political formula in the two countries.

Ms. TITUS. Ms. Dalton, or Ambassador?

Ambassador HOF. I would say, Congresswoman, there is—the
United States does have a—definitely an image and a perception
problem in Syria. It was not born with the executive order. Okay?
It goes back. It goes back a few years. Expectations that the
Obama administration, for example, would do something short of
invading and occupying the country to protect Syrian civilians from
mass murder. The fact that that never happened, unintended con-
sequence for sure, but it does bear on our reputation in the country.

My organization, the Atlantic Council, recently published what I
consider to be a very, very important nonpartisan bipartisan effort.
Steve Hadley and former secretary Madeleine Albright have published a Middle East Strategy Task Force report. And what comes
through clearly in this report is the absolute need we and our
transatlantic partners have for partnerships within the region.

Ultimately, if terror is going to be killed and kept dead in the
Middle East, it is going to be Muslims in the lead. All right? And
again, nobody begrudges the President of the United States, his au-
thorities, his views about the national security of the United
States, but when we do these things, I think—I think we have to
keep in mind the imperative of partnership in the region, who our
partners need to be. And I suspect the administration will be doing
a better job in that respect.

Ms. TITUS. Thank you. Ms. Dalton.

Ms. DALTON. I would completely align myself with Ambassador
Hof's remarks in terms of the necessity of reaching out, not only
to our traditional partners, but also civil society organizations on
the ground. The best messenger of countering violent extremism is
local actors, local religious leaders, community activists. They are
credible in the eyes of the people that we are trying to reach. And
I think bolstering resourcings for those efforts through third-party
means is exceptionally important. And really creating a coalition of
not just government to government but also public-private partnerships also must be part of the equation.

Ms. TITUS. Thank you.

I yield back.

Mr. POE. I thank the gentlelady.

The Chair recognizes the gentleman from Pennsylvania, Mr. Perry.

Mr. PERRY. Thank you, Mr. Chairman.

Ambassador Hof, thanks for your service. In 2015, ICE, Immigration and Customs Enforcement, reported through their intelligence sources that ISIS had been able to co-opt or to obtain passport information data, biometric data, facilities, equipment, et cetera, in Syria, and they were able to falsify or manufacture passports in that regard with that information.

I am just wondering, since that time, this is the end of 2015, as I understand it and as I recall it, did we ever verify that? And does ISIS or al-Qaeda, for that matter, currently maintain access to Syrian Government facilities, equipment, biometric data, passport information, et cetera, that would allow either one of those groups to forge passports and/or falsify identities? Anybody?

Mr. HASSAN. Sure. Just quickly. I think the only place that, you know, people inside Syria talked about with little evidence was Aleppo, but ISIS did not go to Aleppo. So if there was another—if there was one group that took the—you know, seized these ones, it wouldn't be ISIS. It would be Free Syrian Army groups.

Mr. PERRY. But involved in the Free Syrian Army—I mean, we have a hard time, I think, distinguishing who's who, and it changes, in some respects, seems to be month to month or if you want to say year to year. Could those—that information have fallen into the hands of al-Qaeda or al-Qaeda operatives, even if they weren't particularly ISIS operatives?

Mr. HASSAN. I can't say, to be honest.

Mr. PERRY. Based on that, I mean, and maybe in conjunction with that, I mean, what confidence should the United States Government have in the Government of Syria and the actors in Syria to accurately confirm the identities of immigrants or refugees from Syria?

Ambassador HOF. Congressman, my sense, and I am certainly not an expert in consular affairs, my sense is that there is a very intensive and very long vetting process for Syrian refugees to come to the United States. My suspicion is that the administration will probably find some tweaks, if you will, to improve that on the margins, but my—again, not being a consular specialist, you know, my sense from people who are in this business is that Syrian refugees considered to come to the United States get a pretty thorough scrubbing.

Mr. PERRY. I am not doubting at all the capabilities, the diligence, et cetera, of the people in the United States doing the vetting. What I am questioning or trying to determine is the validity of the information that they compare against, who is giving it to them, what their interests may be, those who are giving the information, and the validity and the competence in the validity of that information coming from—does all that information come from the Assad Government or is there anybody else providing information? If you don't know, you don't know, but I am just—you know, looking at the map, I mean, obviously there is a lot of different players, right?

So when a refugee comes from here, are they getting the information from Damascus, they being the United States, to vet this person, or is somebody in this region or any of these other regions providing some form of governance or tyranny or whatever you want to call it—where is that information coming from? Do we know? Do you know?

Ambassador HOF. Congressman, speaking for myself, I don't know. Syrian refugees in Turkey, Lebanon, Jordan, elsewhere in Europe who apply to come to the United States have, in most cases, documentation from the Syrian Government: Passport, I.D., and so forth. That, I think, is where the investigation starts.

There are numerous, numerous agencies of the United States Government involved in this, numerous international organizations as well. And I, although I don't know, I strongly suspect that the kinds of questions that you are putting your finger on as to the validity of basic identity documents probably rates high in these investigations.

Mr. PERRY. Thank you, Ambassador.

Mr. Chairman, I yield.

Mr. POE. I thank the gentleman.

Ms. Dalton, I understand that you need to leave. There may be questions that members of the committee have not been able to ask you and they may turn those in in writing, which will be forwarded to you, and we would expect you to answer those questions within a week of when you received them. With that understanding, then you can leave.

Ms. DALTON. Thank you so much, Chairman. And I beg the subcommittee's forgiveness. I have a flight to catch today, but thank you so much for the opportunity to testify, and I would be glad to answer any followup questions. Thank you.

Mr. POE. Thank you, Ms. Dalton.

Mrs. Torres, you probably had all your questions for Ms. Dalton, but you are recognized.

Mrs. TORRES. Absolutely, but that is okay. Thank you so much, Mr. Chairman.

Terrorism, in many ways, is fueled by poverty and poor governance. In the long run, if Syria doesn't see better governance and prosperity, then even if ISIS is defeated, something else will take its place.

Getting back, Ambassador Hof, to, you know, what you were trying to get at earlier when you said, you know, who should our partners in the region be, who should we be working with there, I wonder if you can sort of look at your crystal ball, 5 years from now, down the road, you know, what are the prospects for the Syrian economy and Government? Will the Syrian economy and Government be better off if Russia and Iran are in the main outside powers shaping events in Syria, or should—what would that look like if the U.S. and Europe are the main outside powers shaping events in Syria?

Ambassador HOF. Thank you for your—thank you for your question, Congresswoman. I would say off the top of my head that if Iran, in particular, is playing a decisive role 5 years from now in Syria, Syria will be basically a smoking pit, and it will be hemorrhaging human beings in all directions.

Iran—Iran needs Bashar al-Assad for one thing and one thing only. He is—he and his entourage are the only people in a very nationalistic country willing to subordinate Syria 100 percent to Iran on the issue of Hezbollah. Iran knows there is nobody else in the country willing to go that far. So from Iran's point of view, it is Bashar or nothing.

Now, there are estimates out there that the rebuilding of Syria is going to take something on the order of $350 billion worth of investment, in some cases aid, grants. We are not even talking about humanitarian assistance here. Reconstruction. Okay? And there is a practical problem here, and I think the Russians get this, okay, because the Russians know the Assad regime probably better than any of us.

Mrs. TORRES. But do they understand the rule of law?

Ambassador HOF. I don't think that is a—I don't think that is a high priority. I think—I think what the Russians do understand is it is going to be very difficult for international financial institutions, for the United States, for Japan, for Western Europe to make the kinds of investment, make the kinds of grants and loans if you have got Bashar al-Assad and his entourage sitting there with their hands cupped ready to take a piece of this.

Now, you know, as an American, like everybody else here, I am— I guess I am basically an optimist. Yes, 5 years from now I do see Syria in a much better place, but that—that is going to require very, very, very strong efforts for all of us. There is a formula out there for moving toward a national unity governing scheme. It was agreed in June 2012 by Russia, China, the United States, Great Britain, and France. Our diplomatic challenge right now, I think, is to try to convince the Russians to get that back on track.

Mrs. TORRES. But meanwhile, you know, we have thousands of people that are—continue to be slaughtered in the region and with very little control. You, yourself, stated that there is very little protection in some of these camps for folks. What more can be done to get our regional partners involved, if not Russia?

Ambassador HOF. I think—I think for all of our regional partners there is a—there is an obligation that needs to be met in terms of providing sufficient funds for the humanitarian assistance that needs to take place. Thanks to you ladies and gentlemen and your colleagues in the appropriations process, the American taxpayer has been very generous in this respect.

Mrs. TORRES. Thank you.

And I yield back.

Mr. POE. I thank the gentlelady.

The Chair recognizes the gentleman from Virginia, Mr. Garrett.

Mr. GARRETT. Thank you, Mr. Chairman.

Mr. Hassan, I want to clear up the record based on some questions asked by my colleague from Pennsylvania, Mr. Perry. He queried you whether or not there might have been access to equipment in Aleppo that might allow individuals to forge Syrian passports, official documents, and your response, as I recall, was that ISIS was not in Aleppo, that that was the Free Syrian Army. Is it not also true, however, that a significant faction in Aleppo was Jabhat al-Nusrah or Jabhat Fatah al-Sham?

Mr. HASSAN. Inside Aleppo, Jabhat al-Nusrah Arpar was never dominant. That was true until it was expelled—until the Russians and the regime expelled the rebels from Aleppo.

Mr. GARRETT. Okay. But there were factions of Jabhat al-Nusrah and Jabhat Fatah al-Sham in Aleppo, correct?

Mr. HASSAN. Absolutely.

Mr. GARRETT. And Aleppo was, prior to this upheaval, the largest city in the nation and a seat for a significant amount of government activity, correct?

Mr. HASSAN. Yes. Remember, this was in 2012, and the jihadists were not yet there in that sense.

Mr. GARRETT. Well, Mr. Hassan, the people who I have spoken with who were there on the ground indicated that when the Arab Spring occurred, the uprising was of individuals who had dissatisfaction with the regime but not necessarily an intent to overthrow. Ultimately, that leadership was co-opted or even killed and replaced by elements affiliated with al-Qaeda, originally known as al-Nusrah, right, and then an evolution of names.

I guess what I am driving at is, the answer to Mr. Perry's question was, if they controlled the proper parts of Aleppo, al-Qaeda-affiliated elements may have had access to equipment that could be used to forge government documents. And they were in Aleppo, were they not?

Mr. HASSAN. In all honesty, I can't tell, because I have no—I have not—I have no evidence to that or the contrary. But it is all possible. The regime still had presence inside Aleppo, so the equipment would have been taken very quickly to the west side of Aleppo where the regime was there. There was rumors that—there were rumors that some biometrics machines were still there.

Mr. GARRETT. And we know that there were elements of what was originally al-Nusrah, which is morphed into an al-Qaeda affiliate, that were in control of portions of Aleppo over periods of time.

Mr. HASSAN. Yes, lately.

Mr. GARRETT. Okay. I wished that Ms. Dalton didn't have to leave. We have talked a lot, and her comment was, "our objectives are not aligned with those of Russia." What would either of you gentlemen or both articulate as our objectives?

Ambassador HOF. I would say, Congressman, our principal objective is to defeat terror in Syria and keep it dead. This is—this is a national security objective, okay. Part of that involves going after ISIL directly militarily as quickly as possible. This organization has been sitting in its Syrian capital of Raqqa for a few years now. It has planned and executed some major atrocities in Europe. I mean, I have been asking myself, you know, for quite some time now how lucky do we think we are, okay. But killing that organization is one thing. Ultimately, there has to be something resembling decent, responsive, legitimate governance in Syria to keep it dead, and this is going to be the work of several years.

Mr. GARRETT. So I don't want to be disrespectful, and I appreciate your time, but I have limited time. So our objective is decent, responsible government in Syria that will protect Syrians. Okay. And right now, there—you can see that the vast bulk of, quote, anti-Assad military power on the ground is Kurdish in nature if you extract ISIS and al-Qaeda-affiliated elements. Combat power on the ground, we both served, that aside from ISIS and al-Qaeda-affiliated elements, the most powerful player that is "anti-Assad is the Kurds."

Ambassador HOF. I would say, Congressman, the Kurdish military power on the ground in Syria, the YPG, this is predominantly our ground combat component against ISIL. They are not—they are not fighting—they are not fighting the regime.

Mr. GARRETT. I agree, and that is why I used quotes when I said anti-Assad, because they are included on this form as anti-Assad. They are really pro-protecting themselves. And we have had wonderful success working with Kurdish minorities, but one thing we have learned is the Kurdish minorities protect Kurdish regions and then say why are we going this direction, right. And so the question becomes, and I know I am almost out of time, who is the viable entity to replace the Assad regime, because it is not ISIS or al-Qaeda? So who is there that can do it?

Ambassador HOF. Congressman, there is—there is—there is a process, again, that was agreed to by the permanent five members of the Security Council on June 30, 2012. I was there as part of the American delegation when this agreement was reached.

If we can somehow get back to that process in forming a national unity entity that will include, inevitably, members of the Syrian Government, you know, who are not—who are not covered in blood over the past few years, if we can get that way, that is—that is the beginning of the end for terrorism in Syria.

Mr. GARRETT. Mr. Chairman, I respect that my time is up.

Mr. POE. All right. The gentleman's time is expired.

The Chair recognizes the gentlelady from Florida, Ms. Frankel.

Ms. FRANKEL. Thank you, Mr. Chairman. I will be quick. I have to go to another meeting.

Thank you both for your testimony, and I just wanted to make two points. I think it was Ms. Dalton, but maybe somebody else, that talking about the necessity, perhaps, of making some type of deal or cooperative arrangement or using sanctions against Russia in order to influence Assad. And I think this paper we were given just shows there is such a complicated web of players, andunraveling it is a phenomenal exercise.

But I want to say that if we are going to have any hope of working with Russia, then I want to respectfully suggest that this Congress needs to know the relationship of Russia to the folks currently in the White House. And the resignation today of General Flynn, I think, calls in serious question as to what exactly who knew what, what did they know, when did they know it, and what is the real relationship between the White House and Russia. That is number one.

Number two, I think it was the Ambassador that said—called what was going on in Syria a humanitarian abomination. And was that you, sir? Yes. I agree with you. I think everybody here agrees with you. I think our chairman laid out initially in his remarks the horrors of what is going on. And I can just say this, I heard the sadness in your heart of what is going on. What is it, ½ million people probably killed, 50,000 children, the President bombing his own people.

And so I wanted to say what I think is another abomination, and that is the position of the United States of America that we do not want to take any of these Syrian refugees into this country. I think that is an abomination. And I yield back.

Mr. Poe. I thank the gentlelady.

And the Chair recognizes the gentleman from California, Mr. Rohrabacher.

Mr. Rohrabacher. Thank you very much, Mr. Chairman.

Let me get to the nitty-gritty. First of all, this is a hearing that is represented by think tanks. One of the think tanks, she had to leave, but let me ask this: Do either of your think tanks receive contributions from Gulf State countries?

Ambassador Hof. Sir, the case of the Hariri Center for the Middle East, we receive no government funding at all.

Mr. Rohrabacher. Or from private sector people from the Middle East?

Ambassador Hof. Our principal donor is of Lebanese citizenship residing in Europe.

Mr. Rohrabacher. A Lebanese citizen?

Ambassador Hof. Yes.

Mr. Rohrabacher. And what about from your think tank?

Mr. Hassan. No government money.

Mr. Rohrabacher. No Arab money comes from——

Mr. Hassan. Not that I am aware of, no.

Mr. Rohrabacher. Okay. And where does your money come from?

Mr. Hassan. Oh, Arab, sorry, and Egypt, yes.

Mr. Rohrabacher. But Arab money, yes.

Mr. Hassan. Egyptian businessman, the principal——

Mr. Rohrabacher. And what Arab money goes into your——

Mr. Hassan. Just Egypt.

Mr. Rohrabacher. Who?

Mr. Hassan. Egypt.

Mr. Rohrabacher. Oh, Egypt. I didn't know Egypt had enough money to send over here. We just got back from there.

Mr. Hassan. Not the government.

Mr. Rohrabacher. Not the government. All right.

Well, thank you. Let me just note that I have just got some specific questions for you. If Assad—if we are going to compare Assad, this brutal horrible man, to the other countries in the Gulf, Qatar, Saudi Arabia, even UAE, or now we are finding maybe Erdogan in Turkey. We know the Iranians are very brutal. But if, let's say, with Qatar, let's use that as an example, if there was an uprising against the royal family in Qatar and it was financed by people from the outside trying to overthrow, basically, an insurgency to overthrow the royal family and replace it with, of course, let's say you have all of those nine out of ten people in Qatar are guest workers, let's say they are declaring themselves for ISIL, and they get some support from the outside like that, basically, do you think that the Government of Qatar or these other governments would be less bloody than Assad when Assad was faced with an insurgency movement in his country? Either one of you. These are more benevolent than Assad?

Ambassador HOF. I would say—I would say, Congressman, that I would find it very, very hard to imagine anyone else in the region adopting a political survival strategy that focuses almost exclusively on civilians——

Mr. ROHRABACHER. On what?

Ambassador HOF. On civilians and on civilian terror.

Mr. ROHRABACHER. Uh-huh.

Ambassador HOF. Okay. I think, you know, whether we look at the Independent International Commission of Inquiry and its work, if we—if we—if we look at the work of major American NGOs——

Mr. ROHRABACHER. I cut what you—reclaiming my time.

Ambassador HOF [continuing]. I think the record is clear.

Mr. ROHRABACHER. I have got 5 minutes. How about you? Do you think these other countries are more benevolent than Assad?

Mr. HASSAN. To be honest, I don't think they would do the same.

Mr. ROHRABACHER. They wouldn't do the same.

Mr. HASSAN. What happened in Syria never happened.

Mr. ROHRABACHER. I am sorry, but I have got a limited number of time. You both think that these powerful forces that have—that are armed to the teeth would permit an insurrection to succeed in their countries and not utilize their weapons to destroy and obliterate anyone who is supporting the insurgency. I think you are wrong. We will leave that to whoever is listening to this and reading the transcript.

We have ½ million people who have been dead. Many of them are refugees, there is no doubt about that. There are, of course, a lot of people who are dead who became refugees and survived who are leaving and fleeing ISIL, wasn't it? I mean, didn't we have the ISIL people at the same time murdering Christians by lining them up, and in the grossest fashion, cutting off their heads and engaged in—yes, bombing people from the air is brutal and kills children, et cetera. Cutting people's heads off is a way to frighten large numbers of people and turn them into refugees. We know that happened.

I don't have to tell you, I do not see—I do not believe that this regime and Assad's regime is any different than the rest of the regimes that I have seen for the last 28 years. And there is no reason why—you stated when we asked what our objective is. Our objective is to eliminate these terrorists? No, terrorism and the terrorist forces there. What we have done is our major focus is getting rid of Assad when, in fact, it should be eliminating the ability of the terrorist forces in that region to commit acts that threaten our security, and we have not done that.

Instead, by focusing instead on one dictatorial regime as compared to all the rest of those authoritarian and brutal regimes that exist in that area of the woods, one regime has to go, and our focus is on getting rid of that regime. That makes no sense to me. It is not in our interest any more than it would be in our interest if another regime was under attack by an insurgency from its own people.

And in this case, let us not forget this insurgency has gone on and on and on. The amount of death that has happened has happened because we and others have given the Assad—insurgents against Assad the idea that we are going to give them the means to succeed. And I will have to say that you are repeating. We have to go back to agreement made by outsiders, outside powers way back in 2012. I am sure that gives all of those people who are fighting Assad a reason to keep on going rather than ending this struggle. And if it ends with Assad still in power, I don't think it is going to be any different than having the royal family in Qatar or UAE or Iran or Saudi Arabia or now even Erdogan in Turkey remain in power.

So with that said, thank you, Mr. Chairman.

Mr. POE. I thank the gentleman.

And the subcommittee is adjourned. I thank the witnesses for being here.

[Whereupon, at 4:07 p.m., the subcommittee was adjourned.]

A P P E N D I X

Material Submitted for the Record

SUBCOMMITTEE HEARING NOTICE
COMMITTEE ON FOREIGN AFFAIRS
U.S. HOUSE OF REPRESENTATIVES
WASHINGTON, DC 20515-6128

Subcommittee on Terrorism, Nonproliferation, and Trade
Ted Poe (R-TX), Chairman

TO: MEMBERS OF THE COMMITTEE ON FOREIGN AFFAIRS

You are respectfully requested to attend an OPEN hearing of the Committee on Foreign Affairs, to be held by the Subcommittee on Terrorism, Nonproliferation, and Trade in Room 2172 of the Rayburn House Office Building (and available live on the Committee website at http://www.ForeignAffairs.house.gov):

DATE: Tuesday, February 14, 2017

TIME: 2:00 p.m.

SUBJECT: Defeating Terrorism in Syria: A New Way Forward

WITNESSES: Mr. Hassan Hassan
                  Senior Fellow
                  The Tahrir Institute for Middle East Policy

                  The Honorable Frederic C. Hof
                  Director
                  Rafik Hariri Center for the Middle East
                  Atlantic Council

                  Ms. Melissa Dalton
                  Senior Fellow
                  Center for Strategic and International Studies

By Direction of the Chairman

The Committee on Foreign Affairs seeks to make its facilities accessible to persons with disabilities. If you are in need of special accommodations, please call 202/225-5021 at least four business days in advance of the event, whenever practicable. Questions with regard to special accommodations in general (including availability of Committee materials in alternative formats and assistive listening devices) may be directed to the Committee.

COMMITTEE ON FOREIGN AFFAIRS

MINUTES OF SUBCOMMITTEE ON ___*Terrorism, Nonproliferation, and Trade*___ HEARING

Day___*Tuesday*___ Date___*February 14, 2017*___ Room_____*2172*_____

Starting Time___*2:01 p.m.*___ Ending Time___*4:07 p.m.*___

Recesses |__*1*__| (_*2:26 p.m.*_ to _*3:10 p.m.*_) (____to____) (____to____) (____to____) (____to____) (____to____)

Presiding Member(s)

Chairman Ted Poe

Check all of the following that apply:

Open Session ☑
Executive (closed) Session ☐
Televised ☑

Electronically Recorded (taped) ☑
Stenographic Record ☑

TITLE OF HEARING:

"Defeating Terrorism in Syria: A New Way Forward"

SUBCOMMITTEE MEMBERS PRESENT:

Reps. Poe, Keating Wilson, Frankel, Cook, Titus, Perry, Torres, Zeldin, Schneider, Mast, Garrett

---

NON-SUBCOMMITTEE MEMBERS PRESENT: *(Mark with an * if they are not members of full committee.)*

Rohrabacher

HEARING WITNESSES: Same as meeting notice attached? Yes ☑ **No** ☐
(If "no", please list below and include title, agency, department, or organization.)

STATEMENTS FOR THE RECORD: *(List any statements submitted for the record.)*

SFR - "Syria - Areas of Control" map submitted by Chairman Ted Poe

---

TIME SCHEDULED TO RECONVENE_____
or
TIME ADJOURNED___*4:07 p.m.*___

Subcommittee Staff Associate

48

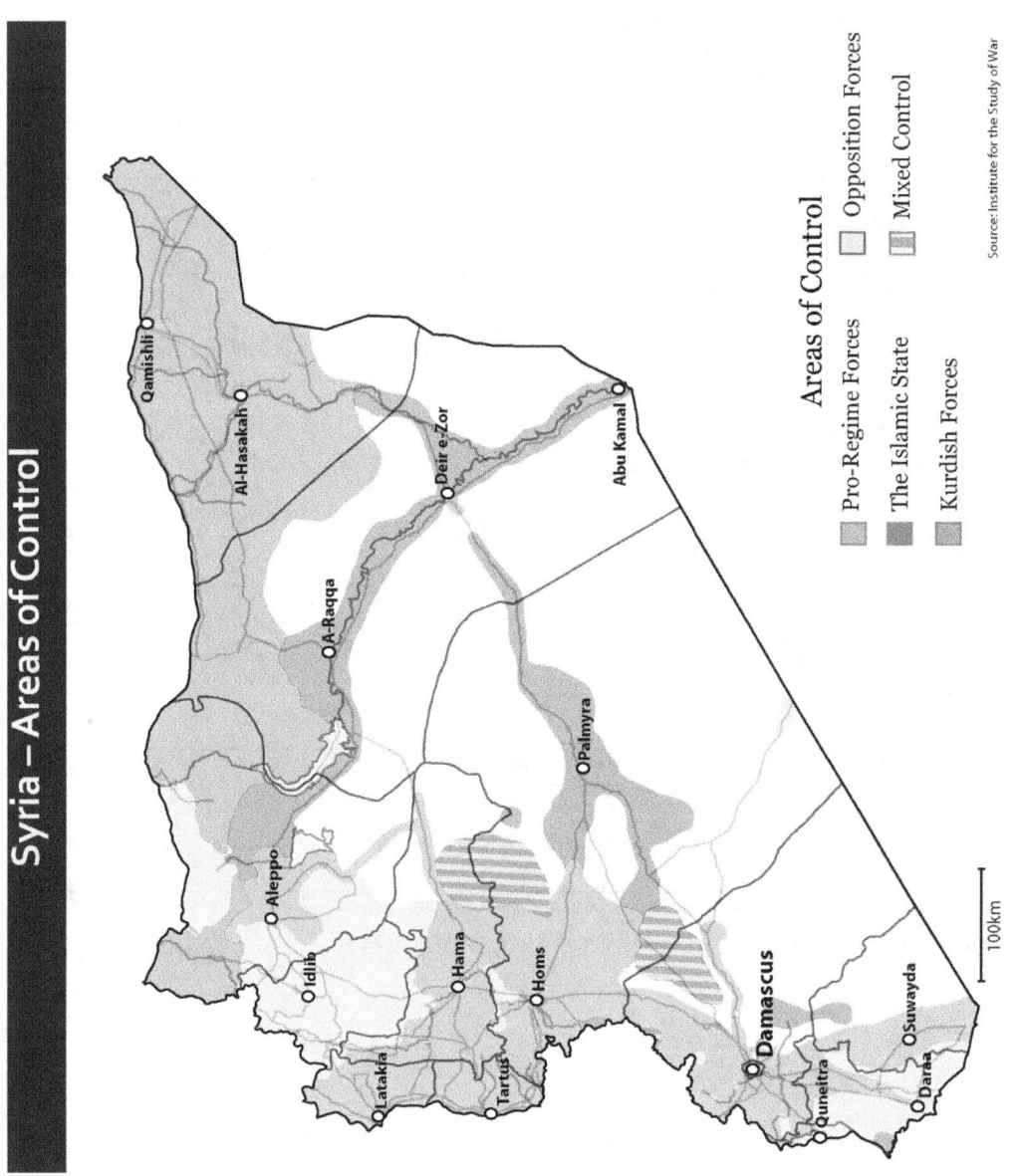